W9-BXM-132

GETTING

RICH

WITH

OPM*

The Fine Art of
Personal Leverage

*OTHER PEOPLE'S MONEY

GETTING RICH WITH OPM*

The Fine Art of
Personal Leverage

PAUL SARNOFF

*OTHER PEOPLE'S MONEY

PARKER PUBLISHING COMPANY, INC.

West Nyack, New York

GETTING RICH WITH OPM*

The Fine Art of
Personal Leverage

*Other People's Money

by

Paul Sarnoff

© 1971, BY

PARKER PUBLISHING COMPANY, INC.
WEST NYACK, NEW YORK

LIBRARY OF CONGRESS
CATALOG CARD NUMBER: 74-152524

PRINTED IN THE UNITED STATES OF AMERICA
ISBN 0-13-354753-1
B & P

To my Stevie

How This Book Can Help
Increase Your Income

This book focuses precisely on the kind of specialized financial knowledge already quite familiar to most millionaires and successful investors. The key lies in the skillful use of OPM—Other People's Money. After acquiring the practical information this book will emphasize, you will be well on the path toward successful application of corporate credit principles to personal financial matters, such as generating extra cash and planning levered equity risks. It is my belief that if people planned their financial operations in the manner that big business does, they would reap the extra rewards that corporations receive when they make proper and effective use of other people's money.

You will find here the secrets of successful stock market speculators and be able to apply leverage strategies that could accelerate profits in stocks, bonds, real property and commodities. Naturally, the application of leverage in any situation that involves price change requires the use of sound knowledge and careful judgment. Leverage, of course, heightens the eventual profits when you are right, and again, this book is designed to help increase the probability of your developing a sound basis for each decision.

Another advantage of the book is that it deals with one aspect of financial operations that could not only be time-saving, but downright intriguing: *there is no need to be a financial wizard.* Everything you need to know will be found in this book.

There is still another important advantage: *you do not need to have a substantial sum to invest.* Quite the contrary, the whole point in developing the power of personal leverage is to secure and *use* funds from other sources that will work toward increasing your own personal wealth. You will learn many ways to secure this leverage and apply it toward a variety of investment possibilities. Some are quite unique, and all offer the potential of solid financial profit.

Let us now proceed toward developing a clear understanding of this "fine art." If you learn the lessons in leverage included throughout the book—and apply them intelligently toward earning extra profits from your effort—my labors will have been worthwhile . . . and you will make money.

PAUL SARNOFF

Table of Contents

PREFACE 7

Chapter 1. THE POWER OF PERSONAL
LEVERAGE 15

*Trading on the Equity . . . The Cash
Flow Projection . . . Leveraged Profit-
Power . . . Who Is Rich? . . . Leverage
Makes the Difference . . . Those Added
Risks . . . Double Your Money . . . Some
Credit Loopholes . . . Perfect Leverage
. . . Liquidity Paradox . . . Leverage
Logic . . . Foreign Trades.*

Chapter 2. LEVERAGE-LADEN MEDIA . . . 31

*About Warrants . . . Put-and-Call Lever-
age . . . Fortunes in Futures . . . Rights
Power . . . A Special Subscription . . .
Warrants Checklist . . . The Put-and-
Call "Bible" . . . Call Power . . . The
Leverage Summary.*

Chapter 3. SOURCES OF LEVERAGE 45

*The Mother-in-Law Game . . . Special-
Purpose Loans . . . Foreign Leverage . . .
Day Trading . . . Free Riding . . . Draft
Delivery . . . Foreign Accounts . . . The
Borrowed Money Game . . . The Loss
Factor . . . House Rules.*

9

Chapter 4. THE POWER OF PYRAMID-
ING 65

*Buying Power . . . Generating Cash . . .
Pyramid Power . . . Account Switching
Leveraged Triple Play . . . Leveraged
Prudence.*

Chapter 5. COMMODITIES—AND PER-
SONAL LEVERAGE 75

*The Hedging Habit . . . Those Active
Commodities . . . A Market of Price Pat-
terns . . . Inflation Factor . . . Pyramiding
Media . . . Commodity Specialists . . .
Special Margin Dispensations . . . The
Cutten Case.*

Chapter 6. COW DEALS 89

*Feed-Lot Fortunes . . . A Typical Cow
Club . . . Stock Split in Beef . . . Banking Help.*

Chapter 7. CONVERSION POWER 97

*Listed Leverage . . . Conversion Power
. . . Sell a Put: Buy a Call . . . OTC
Strategy . . . About Extensions.*

Chapter 8. THE HOARDERS 111

*Those Silver Certificates . . . Coins Mean
Extra Cash . . . Oh! Those Cartwheels
. . . Profits from Hoarding . . . About
Antiques . . . Vineyard Profits . . . The
Art Mania.*

Chapter 9. PROFITS—WITH PROTEC-
TION 125

Price Protection ... Stock Market Insurance ... Protected Leverage ... Downside Insurance.

Chapter 10. LEVERAGING THE MONEY
MARKET **133**

Debt Instrument Mix ... Those Treasury Bills ... A Case in Governments ... Currency Hedging ... Inflation Dollars ... Money Market Pros.

Chapter 11. REAL ESTATE LEVERAGE. . . **147**

Find a Property ... Development Fortunes ... Mortgage Recasting ... Building a Second Income ... Real Property —And Banks ... Form a Team ... Political Help ... Delicate Matters ... You Can't Manufacture Land.

Chapter 12. LEVERAGED RETIREMENT . . **159**

Earning Power ... About Older People ... Sensible Financial Planning.

Chapter 13. REAR-VIEW LEVERAGE **165**

20/20 Hindsight ... Comeback Stocks ... Make It with Bonds ... Tax Loss Benefits.

GLOSSARY **173**

INDEX **189**

GETTING
RICH
WITH
OPM*

The Fine Art of
Personal Leverage

*OTHER PEOPLE'S MONEY

· · · · 1 · · · ·

The Power of
Personal Leverage

Billy Rose once called to tell me he intended to acquire a huge block of New York Central stock. In his dry, matter-of-fact voice he further confided, "I'm buying all I can borrow...."

At the time, Billy needed to borrow money about as much as a Bedouin needs a surfboard. Yet the "Bantam Barnum" unhesitatingly hocked his assets to buy —on credit—500,000 shares of Central. Shortly afterward he repeated the process with a margined purchase of 400,000 Pennsylvania.

Why?

Like so many other successful latter-day money managers, Billy clearly understood the awesome power of personal leverage to build *extra* profits—not only in the stock market, but also in real estate and other equities. Yes, Billy Rose indeed knew how to promote his fortune by using OPM (Other People's Money) to make more money for himself. But what is personal leverage? And how can anyone use this power intelligently and sensibly to make extra profits for himself?

Trading on the Equity

As most business people already know, leverage is the application of credit—some call it trading on the equity—to present and future corporate operations. In this regard, the leverage-minded business manager seeks sources of short, medium and long-term funds. He creates what is known as a financial mix, staggering maturities of his company's borrowings to fit in comfortably with its ability to generate cash to meet its outstanding commitments. And why do even the most affluent businesses borrow? Because they have the ability to make money on the funds they seek. For example, American Telephone and Telegraph Company, probably the best financially managed corporation in the world, eagerly went into the capital markets in early 1968 to borrow $250 million in debentures (bonds) with an interest rate of 6 per cent. "Big Telephone's" wisdom became quite evident as the year wore on and corporate interest rates zoomed over 7 per cent. Even if AT&T did nothing with the borrowed funds but lend them back into the capital markets, they could have earned a handsome return, for during 1969 the Government itself. floated 18-month notes bearing interest rates of 8 per cent!

How often in academe is a corporation likened to a human being—with the "blood" of the corporation, of course, being its "cash flow." And oddly enough, our tax structure favors corporations over individuals. But instead of belaboring what we feel are tax abuses, it is more fitting to attempt to inculcate an aura of professionalism in personal-risk transactions by emulating certain aspects of corporate financial operations and management. In other words, an investor should appraise both his present and future earnings—together with his reserves—in the same manner that corporate managers assess a company's future. Moreover, the individual investor should employ *financial management* in his investment operations. By financial management, of course, we mean a forward-looking inquiry based upon a sound view of the past.

The Cash Flow Projection

For example, an executive may be netting, after expenses and taxes, $10,000 a year; and his future for the next ten years seems secure. Thus it is reasonable to project a cash flow for the next ten years of such a sum, winding up with an excess of $100,000. Therefore, it makes some sense for this executive to hock himself to the tune of $100,000 for that period if he can effect proper long-term arrangements. Assuredly, borrowing $10,000 or $20,000 isn't too risky with this kind of cash flow. In any event, every investor should draw up a personal balance sheet for his own edification, indicating what he owns on the left-hand-side; what he owes on the right-hand-side and his net worth.

Such a balance sheet for a 35-year-old American-on-the-way-up might be:

Balance Sheet: John Cash, 1971

ASSETS:

Cash in banks	$20,000
Investments	20,000
Real estate (residence)	30,000
Furniture, etc.	5,000
GTO or Cougar	3,500
Stamps, books, art and other collections	3,000
Total assets	$81,500

LIABILITIES:

Mortgage	$15,000
Car loan	2,500
Current bills payable	1,000
Total liabilities	$18,500

NET WORTH:

Assets less liabilities	$63,000

What will John Cash be worth in 1981?
Assuming he nets $10,000 a year after taxes and expenses and is so conservative he keeps this in cash, his projected balance sheet could look something like this:

Balance Sheet: John Cash, 1981

ASSETS:

Cash in banks	$120,000
Investments*	40,000
Real estate*	60,000
Furniture, etc.	5,000
Cadillac or Continental	10,000
Stamps and other collections	15,000
Total assets	$250,000

LIABILITIES:

Mortgage	$8,000
Car loan	8,000

Current bills 3,000

Total liabilities $19,000

NET WORTH:

Assets less liabilities $231,000

---

* Note: Assume investments doubled in value, while collections quintupled.

Leveraged Profit Power

In 1981, probably, John Cash can sit back satisfied that now he has to do some estate planning since his net worth exceeds the $120,000 exemption for a married man under community property will situations. But assume that John Cash had read this book and had become knowledgeable (a nasty word) about personal leverage—and had applied his lessons in leverage properly by generating cash in 1971 to lever his power to invest—he could have found himself in the following situation:

Leveraged Balance Sheet: John Cash, 1971

ASSETS:

Cash in banks $10,000

Investments 60,000

Real estate 80,000

Furniture 5,000

GTO or Cougar 3,500

Stamps, etc. 3,000

Total assets $161,500

LIABILITIES:

Bank loans vs. securities $30,000

Mortgages vs. realty 65,000

Car loan 2,500

Current bills 1,000

Total liabilities $98,500

NET WORTH:

Assets less liabilities $63,000

Note that John Cash reduced his cash in the bank to a sensible sum of $10,000 to meet emergencies. He took the $10,000 in excess cash and used it to invest in convertible debentures, along with the balance of his $20,000 previously allotted for common stock investments. Since modern margin regulations at banks and brokerage firms permit the purchase of listed convertible debentures with only a 50 per cent deposit, John Cash shrewdly put all his investment funds into these media instead of buying stock of the same corporations, for which he would have had to buy either for all cash or on 65 per cent margin. And so his securities investments—aided by the fillip of the $10,000 from his bank account—burgeoned from $20,000 on a previous all-cash basis to $60,000, on margin.

A leverage-minded John Cash would never sit with a residence worth $30,000 that had a mortgage of only $15,000 on it. He would generate another $10,000 by refinancing his home. Armed now with $20,000 of mortgage money he could—after reading Bockl's book*— take on another $50,000 worth of real estate, swelling his realty holdings to $80,000, from $30,000. Watch what happens to John Cash after ten years of leveraging. Assuming that his assets—although in hock—acted percentage-wise the same as they did during the same period when owned for almost all cash, here is how John's situation shapes up in 1981:

---

* Bockl, George, *How to Use Leverage to Make Money in Local Real Estate,* Prentice-Hall, Inc., 1965.

Projected Leveraged Balance Sheet:
John Cash, 1981

ASSETS:

Cash in banks	$110,000
Investments*	120,000
Real estate*	160,000
Furniture, etc.	5,000
Rolls Royce	22,000
Stamps, etc.	15,000
Total assets	$432,000

LIABILITIES:

Broker loans	$30,000
Realty loans	8,000
Car loan	18,000
Bills	3,000
Total liabilities	$59,000

NET WORTH:

Assets less liabilities	$373,000

* Note that as in the cash of John's projected—and conservative—balance sheet, investments and real estate doubled, while stamps, etc., quintupled in value during the ten-year period. Moreover, a leverage-minded John Cash would have long since liquidated the mortgages on his income properties by techniques described in the aforementioned Bockl's book.

Who Is Rich?

Of course what has been presented here is actually a financial fable that more often than not turns out to be true. Who is rich? The answer is a man's wealth cannot be measured properly by what he owns, but rather by what he owes. Financier Feinstein, an exwindow-washer who climbed his way to a fortune from leverage operations, used to say: "A man is rich only when he owes half-a-million dollars."

Perhaps money is often hard to get. And perhaps you have hesitated from embroiling yourself in leveraging stocks, bonds or real property because of the thought that money is hard to get or that you just might not be qualified to effect the kind of call loans that have made so many business executives believe the motto of that friendly bank. The trick, as will be later demonstrated in Chapter 10, depends on how effectively you will be able to melt the average banker's icy reserve.

In the meantime, unless you learn about leverage to your risk operations—be they stocks, bonds, real estate, cartwheels or corn futures —you will lack the potent panacea that so often makes the difference between small profits and vast riches.

Leverage Makes the Difference

After thoroughly studying the fictional examples of a John Cash operation compared with a *leveraged* John Cash operation, it is fitting to point out that credit-minded John Cash sensibly enough deposited his $10,000-a-year excess from earnings in the bank as a safeguard to cushion the $105,000 of broker loans and mortgages he had open. So while he could have, of course, levered his situation into a million dollars or more during the ten-year period by applying the purchasing power of an additional $10,000 a year in his cash flow to more securities and more real estate, John—realizing the risk in operating on credit—built up a cash reserve. Now in 1981, if he so desires, he can either pay off the $38,000 in broker and realty loans and be satisfied with his net worth of $373,000 (assuredly a more satisfactory situation than had he operated on cash and wound up after ten years with only $231,000); or he could take the plunge and again lever his assets so that in the next ten years he would be worth well over a million—if all factors remained favorable.

Those Added Risks

The trouble, of course, is that often both markets and investment prices do not remain favorable. It should be clearly understood that risk-takers who buy on credit will *make much more* than cash buyers if prices are favorable, but stand to *lose* more if they are not. Ironically, that is why rich people are favored over poor in this regard. After all, a person in the 20 per cent income tax bracket bears 80 per cent of a realized investment loss which is not offset by profits, while a person in the 50 per cent bracket bears only 50 per cent of his stock market or real estate mistakes. Moreover, since interest is a normal tax deduction, the poor fellow in the 20 per cent bracket pays 80 cents on every dollar of interest involved in leverage operations, while the affluent man or woman in the 50 per cent bracket has a "partner" (Uncle Sam), who shoulders 50 per cent of the cost of the credit.

Keeping in mind both the added risk of leverage operations and their costs (anywhere from 5 to 24 per cent of the subject investment per year), the neophyte seeker of credit in his investment approach must clearly fix in his mind the superiority of leveraged investments over cash ones. Naturally, there is little point in deriding the cautious cash approach of conservative investors who insist on fully-paid-for-and-worryless stock and realty positions; but the people in our past who have garnered the great fortunes have always accelerated their profits through borrowed money.

Ask any investor what he wants out of Wall Street—or any other street for that mátter—and invariably the answer is "I want to make money." The trouble is that unsophisticated investors who feel Wall Street "owes them a living," hardly ever set a sensible target for themselves. How much do they expect to make with their money? This question hardly ever arises—and assuredly stands way behind the needful ones: "What to buy?" and "When?"

Double Your Money

Let's take an astute investor who happens to learn about a wonder stock at $100 a share from his barber or dentist. As a sensible investor he sets a goal of doubling his risk money for himself; and after an examination of his financial situation decides he can spare $10,000 for this "tip, listed on the New York Stock Exchange." As a leverage student, he now prepares a table of *alternatives* that range from payment-in-full to purchase of 100 shares in question with varying degrees of leverage. This table, reflecting precisely at what point the investor's money will double (without considering commissions and interest charges), reveals:

Double-the-Money-Table: $10,000 Investment
(Disregard Interest)

Payment Method	Amount of Loan	In- vestor's Equity	Value Equity Doubles at→	Stock Price
All cash	None	$10,000	$20,000	$200
70% margin	$3,000	7,000	17,000	170

50%	"	5,000	5,000	15,000	150
25%	"	7,500	2,500	12,500	125
20%	"	8,000	2,000	12,000	120
10%	"	9,000	1,000	11,000	110

Theoretically, now, our hero is hurled between the financial Scylla and Charybdis of buying 100 shares of the tipped stock for all-cash and hoping his shares will run up to $200, or buying 1,000 shares (borrowing $9,000) and hoping the stock will move up a mere ten points in order to double his money before taxes, commissions and interest.

But hold!

As a United States citizen living in the state of New York, how can this investor legally effect a leveraged purchase of these shares without violating current Federal initial-margin regulations of at least 65 per cent of the purchase deposit? And wouldn't it be amazing if he could carry his $10,000 position for a month without laying out a single penny? Even more amazing—but true—is the fact that informed investors can accomplish this without violating existing rules and regulations of our burgeoning bureaucracy.

How?

This book is not a manual for seekers of bootleg credit—or for seekers of sub-rosa financing—but we certainly intend to cover existing loopholes. And to find out how anyone can buy —and carry—stock with 50 cents on the dollar, 20 cents on the dollar, and even without *any* cents on the dollar, you must read on. The same, of course, is true for realty purchases, which can often be handled by experts with very little or no cash at all.

Some Credit Loopholes

As law-abiding citizens, all of us, including the author, must observe existing—and restrictive—credit rules emanating from federal agencies and from the New York Stock Exchange (a very private club operated strictly for the benefit of its members). When dealing with regulated banks and brokers, we are compelled to abide by antiquated, bizarre, arbitrarily unjust and easily side-stepped rulings. But as in every other area of business restriction, the knowing ones have found legal loopholes in these rules that permit them to operate just as though the rules didn't exist. And oddly enough their activities are aided by the rules themselves.

For example, a customer maintaining a cash account at a broker must pay for purchases within seven business days under current regulations. He must pay for them in three days if he buys on credit—and at this writing must deposit margin of at least 65 per cent of the value of the purchase. Yet a sophisticated trader who has established proper bank connections, can order stock at a broker and have it delivered "draft attached" to his bank. When does he actually have to pay for these shares? When they are delivered to the bank, of course. How long does this take? It depends on where the bank is—from four to thirty days. Obviously, with today's snafu's and bottlenecks in brokerage back offices, it is anybody's guess as to when purchased shares will be delivered. Moreover, if the receiving bank is located in another country, Lord knows when payment will be required. As a member of the Havana Stock Exchange "in absentia" my readers can envision the sorrow I felt at Castro's coming; he ruined, inadvertently, the best leverage scheme ever created by man.

Perfect Leverage

Before Castro's advent in 1958, I could buy $50,000 worth of securities in New York and order them sent by draft to my bank in Havana, the Banco Financiero. This would take about 30 days by banana boat. Meanwhile, if the stock rose in price, I could dispose of the shares at another brokerage house and give that house instructions to pick up the shares in Havana— after paying my bank for them. Thus I couid "free ride" for a month (often for much longer periods) without violating any federal rules. In other words, I had the profit power (the loss potential too) of a stock purchase without putting up any money. This is *perfect leverage*, a rare and sometime thing.

Liquidity Paradox

No equities in the world are as liquid, as readily disposable, as stocks listed on the New York Stock Exchange. And logically, the most liquid investments should command the most liberal credit terms. But life in our American investment milieu never follows logic. Here the most *illiquid* equities are favored with the most extravagant credit. Take real estate. An investor can buy houses, taxpayers, income properties, even post offices by depositing anywhere from 10 to 30 cents on the dollar value of the purchase price. But picture the predicament of an investor who buys a $500,000 apartment house, carries it with a $350,000 mortgage and finds he has to get rid of his investment in a hurry, two weeks after title passes. And so intelligent investors, interested in securities rather than real property, resent this archaic favoritism by governing powers and seek accommodation where logic prevails.

And where is that?

Leverage Logic

A clue was provided in the spring of 1968 by University Computing, an ambitious American corporation vainly seeking to swallow up venerable Western Union.

Because federal regulations dictated that listed stock purchases at the time had to be effected with a minimum of 80 per cent of the purchase price as a deposit, University Computing used Eurodollars to do its buying. In other words, UC went abroad and obtained loan money that was beyond the pale of the Federal Reserve —sidestepping the 80 per cent requirement to swing their Western Union purchases with 20 cents on the dollar. Now if such an operation is feasible, legal and proper for an American corporation, why is it not suitable for individual Americans? Logically, it *is*. You don't have to be a foreigner to benefit from the logical—and enlightened—attitudes of foreign brokers. Compare credit terms at foreign banks and brokers with those at American banks and brokers under the column USA in the following table:

**Initial Margin Required in Various Countries
for Listed Stock Purchases**

Investment Media	Canada	Mexico	Switzerland	Nassau	USA
Bonds (Corporate)	10–20%	20%	10%	15%	25%
Debentures	20–30%	25%	20%	25%	50%
Preferred Stock	50%	50%	20%	25%	65%
Common Stock	50%	50%	20–30%	25%	65%
Warrants (Over $5)	50%	50%	25%	25%	65%

As a disabled American war veteran (60%) I feel no twinge of betrayal in suggesting Americans carry their stock purchases in foreign countries, because this will do nothing whatsoever to worsen our already deplorable balance of payments-deficit. After all, the suggested credit operations involve *American* stocks, bonds, warrants, etc.—and *not* by any means foreign equities. So while it may appear to be heresy to my old friends on the Street to suggest leverage-minded investors set up bases for personal operations outside the United States, the advantages of dealing say with Canadian brokers are immediately apparent when inspecting the following table.

Investment Media	American Broker	Canadian Broker
Listed Common Stocks	65% margin	50% margin
"	Round Lot: 100 shs	Round Lot: 25 shs
"	Eligible stocks from $5 up for margin purposes	Eligible stocks from $1 up for margin purposes
"	Commissions Higher from $15 down	Commissions Lower from $15 down
Short Sale	Uptick needed 65% deposit	No uptick needed. 50% deposit

Foreign Trades

The major deterrent that causes hesitation among Americans in using foreign brokers is that there is an arbitrary withholding tax of 30 per cent of dividends received on American shares held in street name at the foreign broker or bank. But since taxes are deductible and since it is readily assumed that readers of this work will honestly pay taxes on dividends and capital gains garnered in their foreign accounts, this doesn't develop into a large stumbling block for leverage-minded traders. It naturally follows, however, that any ardent seeker of credit-packed securities purchases must establish accounts at at least two brokerage houses and two banks, with one brokerage house and one bank being in another country.

But before continuing to develop the theme that it is every American's inalienable right to always operate at the best possible credit terms in order to try to earn the greatest profit for his risk ventures, it is fitting to examine investment media that have built-in leverage—and whose peculiar makeup can accelerate profits even if Americans remain within the traditional 12-mile limit.

· · · · 2 · · · ·

Leverage-Laden Media

Come into the seemingly complex world of rights, warrants, puts and calls—and futures in commodities, silver dollars, orange juice, etc. This is a world formerly ruled by the pros, but rapidly becoming familiar financial territory to investors who do digging and want to enrich themselves with other people's money. Why are these items so laden with profit potential, even more than stocks, bonds and real estate? The answer is they contain *built-in leverage*. By this we mean that a relatively small investment controls a relatively large price swing, created by an increase either in another security, or in the case of commodities futures by an increase in price of said commodities.

About Warrants

Most investors know that warrants—options to subscribe to shares of stock at fixed prices for long periods of time—usually behave in unison with the common stock they signify. But because of price differential between the warrants and the stock, the warrants will move percentage-wise in a greater degree in either direction. Thus if a warrant is trading at $20 and its stock is trading at $60, and the price of the stock moves up to 64, the warrant could very well move up to 24. This move is slightly more than a 6 per cent appreciation in the stock, but it represents a better than 20 per cent appreciation in the warrant. To simplify things, therefore, sophisticated—and leverage-minded—investors have allotted a built-in leverage factor to most warrants of 3-to-1.

Put-and-Call Leverage

Puts and calls are options to sell and to buy respectively 100 shares of a specific stock at a set price for an agreed time period. This period is, of course, generally shorter than the period allotted to most warrants; but because the cost of these puts and calls is expressed in money, rather than in a premium of market points as is the case in warrants, the built-in leverage factor in puts and calls is much greater. For example, a sensible speculator buys a six-month call option on 100 shares of XYZ listed on the New York Stock Exchange and selling for $100 a share. Assume for simplicity that he pays a 10 per cent premium, or $1,000 plus the customary Lindsay-Rockefeller tax of $5. Now for his $1,005 risk, the speculator controls the upside action of $10,000 worth of stock. Thus his built-in leverage factor is 10. In other words, for every dollar of risk he has a tenfold opportunity of appreciation for every point the stock moves up past his original ten-point cost. Inspection of available media with built-in leverage prompts the following table:

BUILT-IN LEVERAGE FACTORS:
VARIOUS MEDIA*

Investment Media	*Leverage Factor*
Rights	6
Warrants	3
Puts	8
Calls	10
Futures	7

* The significance of this table is its ability to reflect extra profit potential. If the market is favorable, purchase of warrants should bring three times the profit in the stock, etc.

Fortunes in Futures

Now just imagine how much more profit power would become available if the funds for speculations with built-in leverage media were borrowed instead of the investor's own! To understand this, assume an investor in February of any specific year believes September egg futures will rise in value by Easter—after all, eggs are used at that time on lawns, in cakes and for decorative purposes. Checking the past performance charts of egg futures he finds that with rare exceptions, September eggs have indeed appreciated in price during the period February to April—and he decides to plunge. It only takes a $500 deposit, normally, for anybody to contract in February to buy 15,000 dozen September eggs at the prevailing price of say, 35¢ a dozen. Thus for his $500 deposit, the commodities speculator controls the market action of $5,250 of egg futures, but more importantly he controls the price action of 15,000 dozen eggs.* Thus a rise in price of one cent per dozen is a potential increase in his $500 deposit of $150. Now it is kind of silly for a risk-taker in this kind of thing to disturb his savings. Is it not better to take the passbook to the friendly savings bank or thrift institution and get a passbook, low-interest loan in the amount of $500? Having done so, the speculator is now in the same kind of position that the author of a highly popularized book suggests in his *Save by Borrowing*. Here is a chance to save by *making* money from borrowing.

Assume thereafter that eggs appreciate three cents during the selected risk period of February to April and the contract is closed out by a sale of the futures to somebody else through the broker. Since the cost of the round-turn (buy and sell) of one contract is $36, the gross profit of $450 is reduced to $414—but the speculator has made 90 per cent on somebody else's money. Of course, it is distinctly possible that the pattern of price movement of egg futures in the year any speculator wants to try his expertise may reverse. In that event, the speculator can prevent losing more than his original $500 by entering a stop-loss order of say

---

* Size of egg contracts change. Please check before speculating.

three cents down from his purchase price. Because commodities transactions can be an important part of any leverage-minded person who is interested in gaining accelerated profits from price changes, we have devoted an entire chapter to it elsewhere in this work. In the meantime, it is proper to dwell at more length here on the other media mentioned in the built-in leverage table.

Rights Power

Rights to subscribe to new shares of stock in listed issues have become quite a familiar thing as the companies whose shares are listed for trading on the big board resort to this method of working-capital financing. But not every shareholder who receives—or is entitled to receive—subscription rights desires to add to his holdings in this manner by adding more out-of-pocket money into the treasury of the company whose shares he already owns. Besides, because these rights have value, many shareholders simply dispose of them by selling them when they appear for trading on the Exchange. Most rights last from two to eight weeks in duration and have value right up to the moment of expiration because of the activities of a standby syndicate, which is legally permitted to manipulate the market price of the existing shares in order to induce people to subscribe to the new shares to be sold for capital purposes. This standby syndicate, of course, is a group of brokers and investment bankers that already has assured the capital-seeking company it would "take down" (buy) any shares that were not subscribed for by existing shareholders and people who may have bought the rights for speculation. Empirically, the built-in leverage factor for rights, as indicated by the table, is six—and here is a simplified explanation.

Assume a company on the New York Stock Exchange trading at $100 a share decides to offer rights to shareholders to subscribe to new shares of stock from its authorized supply at $90 a share, with the proviso that existing shareholders would be entitled to subscribe to this stock on the basis of one new share for every ten shares of stock already owned. Obviously the value of the new rights are $1 each, when the stock is trading at $100. Now during the ensuing month that the rights offering is effective, the standby syndicate will maintain the price (stabilize) of the stock at about the $100 level on the downside, but permit it to rise above $100 if there is buying demand for existing shares. Because of this, the stock can rise to 101, 102, etc. This rise immediately is reflected in the value of the rights themselves as they trade. Thus it is not surprising to note that rights which come to the Exchange floor at $1 are soon trading at 1 and 8/32nds (usually values are expressed in fractions of this nature for rights), which, of course is $1.25. Now if the stock rises a point, this is a rise of 1 per cent; but if the rights appreciate by 25¢ from $1, this is a rise of 25 per cent. Because of commission costs (in and out to buy and sell the rights) this fantastic percentage is appreciably reduced—and that is why we arbitrarily apply a leverage factor of six, rather than a perhaps more realistic one of 12 or 25 to rights.

Of course, rights are available on over-the-counter stocks, American Exchange stocks and on foreign issues. But experience indicates it is safest for the speculator to play around with rights on the New York Stock Exchange rather than in other markets. Back in 1955 a Canadian company (an industrial) issued rights to subscribe for new stock. The rights came on the Toronto Exchange at 50 cents, went down to 4 cents and then zoomed to $3. Such situations can give traders heart attacks and are to be avoided. One can readily conjure up the consternation of the recipient of such rights who sold them at say 5 cents a right and then watched them trade (three days later) at $2, or forty times the value he received for his property!

A Special Subscription

Another aspect—and a highly useful one for investors, not speculators—is the actual usage of rights to subscribe for shares on a more highly leveraged basis than permissible if the shares themselves were initially purchased. This can be accomplished in what is called a "special subscription account." In this kind of account, the investor buys and pays for rights to subscribe to new shares and exercises those rights —through his broker—by paying only a 25 per cent deposit of the value of the shares he decides to subscribe to. Thus the informed investor can buy subscription stock with a 25 per cent margin as against the investor who may enter the market and buy existing shares of the same issue with a 70 per cent required margin. The cost to the investor is about the same whether he buys rights and subscribes, or whether he merely buys his shares in the same issue on the Exchange, but the *leverage factor* differs. He can swing a purchase in a subscription account with about 30% (figure 5 per cent for cost of rights and commissions for rights, and 25 per cent required deposit), while if he bought the same issue on the open market he would have to put up 65 per cent. Of course, the customer who buys via a special subscription account cannot carry his position longer than three months in that status. All dividends received are applied to his debit balance and he is required to pay for the shares in full within a year by making three more 25 per cent payments. Naturally, the subscription buyer can transfer his shares, when 65 per cent are paid for, into his regular general, or margin, account. But in the meantime—and at least for three months— he has an opportunity to benefit from the 75% leverage in his subscription account. It should be noted, however, that since the subscriber only deposits initially 25 per cent to buy his subscription stock, he is subject to *immediate* margin calls if the shares decline after the rights subscription is over and stabilization by the standby syndicate has ended.

Warrants Checklist

At the start of this chapter we alluded to the leverage power of making money with warrants. In days before a certain advisory service effected a killing for themselves by advertising advice about warrants, some warrants sold at a discount from convertibility and some at a premium. But during the past decade, an artificially created demand by avid speculators for warrants has all but killed their convertibility considerations. Rather, the astute market-player must look at warrants as a means of accelerating profits that could be earned in the underlying stock itself. Because the availability of warrants is rather small and their outstanding number rather thin, the warrants often suffer market convulsions that are greater on both the upside and downside than their underlying stock. In his very fine investor's guide, *Your Investments*, Dr. Leo Barnes provides a table of leading warrants (see page 40). It must be remembered that warrants have no value whatsoever if they have not been resold or exercised (the underlying stock is subscribed for) by expiration date. Moreover, reference to any statistical source such as Standard & Poor's *Stock Guide* will readily reveal the scarcity of the number of warrants available for trading as compared with the number of stock issues. The built-in leverage factor in warrants can be enhanced if the warrants are purchased on credit in margin accounts. And this credit impetus can be even further accelerated by buying a call on a warrant. The possible profit power in this kind of maneuver would be 3×10, or 30.

The Put-and-Call "Bible"

For a complete coverage of puts and calls see the author's book on the subject, Hawthorn Books, 1970. But for this book's purposes it suffices to say that there is no other form of leverage comparable to successful puts and successful calls. In November of 1957, one of my

CHECKLIST: LEADING LONGER TERM WARRANTS CURRENTLY OUTSTANDING★

Warrant	1 war. buys this no. of com.	Current subscription price per share	Expires on	Where traded stock	warrant
Allegheny Corp.	1	3.75	perpetual	NYS	ASE
Allegheny Airlines	1	13.00	4- 1-87	ASE	ASE
Atlas Corp.‡●	1	6.25	perpetual	NYS	ASE
Automatic Retailers	1	41.50	2-28-73	NYS	O-C
Bramalea Consol.	1	10.00	7- 1-73	TOR	O-C
Braniff Airways	1	73.00	12- 1-86	NYS	ASE
Coburn Corp.‡	1	13.13	8-14-79	ASE	O-C
Colonial Acceptance	1	10.00	6-30-74	O-C	O-C
Consol. Leasing	1	5.50	4- 1-73	ASE	O-C
Far West Financial‡	1	21.50	11- 1-79	NYS	O-C
Financial General‡	1.20	15.42	6-15-78	ASE	O-C
Frontier Airlines	1	15.00	3- 1-87	ASE	O-C
Hoerner-Waldorf	1	30.00	10-31-73	ASE	O-C
Husky Oil Can. D	1	10.50	6-30-74	TOR	TOR
Indian Head	1	20.00	5-15-90	NYS	ASE
Intl. Industries	1	15.00	1-31-77	ASE	O-C
McCrory Corp. (New)‡	1	20.00	3-15-81	NYS	ASE
McCrory Corp. (Old)	1	20.00	3-15-76	NYS	ASE
Mid-Amer. Pipeline	1	9.00	3-31-72	NYS	O-C
Midwest. Gas Trans.	1	15.00	12-31-73	O-C	O-C
Natl. General	0.28547	15.65	2-28-74	NYS	O-C
Natl. General $15	1	15.00	5-14-74	NYS	ASE
Pneumo Dynamics	1	11.50	6-30-75	ASE	O-C
Proteus Foods	1	6.00	6-30-77	O-C	O-C
Puritan Fashions	1	13.00	8- 1-81	ASE	O-C
Quebec Nat. Gas '63	1	9.50	6- 1-73	TOR	TOR
Quebec Nat. Gas '66	1	15.00	4-15-76	TOR	TOR
Realty Equities	1.255	7.16	2- 1-72	ASE	ASE
Shell Investments	0.25	80.00	9-30-72	TOR	TOR
Standard Computers	1	13.50	3- 1-80	O-C	O-C
Textron‡	1	15.00	5- 1-84	NYS	ASE
Trans-Canada Pipe Line	1	41.00	4-30-76	TOR	TOR
Trans World Airl.●	1	22.00	12- 1-73	NYS	ASE
Tri-Continental	2.54	8.88	perpetual	NYS	ASE
Uris Bldgs.●	1.0609	11.78	5- 1-75	NYS	ASE
Webb, Del E.‡	1	6.25	12- 1-75	NYS	O-C

‡Indicates that warrant is only partially protected against dilution (see 5, page 144).

●Indicates that the related bond or preferred stock may be used at par value in exercising this warrant (see page 142).

★Issues with fewer than 100,000 warrants outstanding, or where warrants have less than 2 years to run from January 1, 1968, have been automatically excluded from this checklist.

ASE—American Stock Exchange
NYS—New York Stock Exchange
O-C—Over-the-counter
TOR—Toronto Stock Exchange

customers bought a put on 100 B&O at 33¼ for sixty days, for a premium (cost) of $250 (no taxes on puts). Over the following week-end it was announced that B&O's directors had decided to halve the quarterly dividend (from 50¢ to 25¢). The stock fell out of bed and my customer cashed in his put at 23 (he bought stock at 23 and put it to the endorser of the put option at the specified price of 33¼). When the smoke of commissions, etc. blew over, my customer found himself three days later with a clear profit (before his own income taxes, of course) of $700 on his $250 risk—or almost three times on his money. So for readers who feel a stock is too high and may collapse, the best method of taking advantage of this conclusion is to buy *puts*. Costs of puts vary according to the kind of stock and its price action; the costs for calls are somewhat higher, because of inherent benefit from a reduction in the agreed option price due to dividend payouts.*

Sophisticated investors like Barney Baruch and Billy Rose for decades used the leverage advantages in calls to control the price action of thousands of shares of stock, while limiting their own risk. After all, while no one really knows how much profit any specific put or call can bring, everyone should immediately be aware of the limits of his potential loss, which, of course, is the cost of the puts or calls involved. Some stock market risk-takers have been heard to say "Puts and calls are better bets than horse races. You have longer to cheer and get a tax

---

* For a free cost-calculator, write to the author at Lombard Street, Inc., 170 Broadway, New York City, 10038.

deduction if you lose." Whether or not we consider puts and calls stock market bets is not the question. The truth happens to be that using them is the *only* way a trader or investor can call his stock market shots and limit his stock market losses in advance. Ironically, our tax structure favors rich people over poor people in using puts and calls. Obviously, a person paying $1,000 for a call will bear the brunt of the loss if he is in the 20 per cent tax bracket, while a wealthy person in the 50 per cent bracket has the government as an equal partner in his losses. On the profit side the same lopsided situation exists. Rich people can effect long-term gains with calls and pay a maximum of only twenty-five per cent of the profits.

Call Power

Moreover, since calls control roughly ten times their value in stock, the person buying them should realize there is a definite savings in interest that would be lost if funds were used to buy the shares instead of an option on the shares. Thus a call on XYZ at 100 for six months that involves a cost of $1,000 should really be reduced by the interest earned in the bank on the $9,000 that isn't necessary to pay for the stock, while enjoying all its benefits. Considering money as worth say, 8 per cent, this premium actually should be reduced by $360 to a more realistic figure of $640.

It naturally follows that readers who desire to take advantage of profit possibilities in leverage operations must become acquainted both with the plus power of puts and calls and their hedging powers. A put "stops out" all downward deterioration in a long stock position and a call stops out all upside deterioration in an adverse short position. Thus puts and calls can be used also as insurance.

The Leverage Summary

At this point it is fitting to summarize the leverage media and compare the loan possibilities as follows:

Speculative Medium	Maximum Loan Value	Fed. Regulations	Spec. Purpose
Government Obligations	90–95 per cent	95 per cent	90 per cent
Good Listed Bonds	80 per cent	90 per cent	80 per cent
Good Listed Stocks	35 per cent	35 per cent	75 per cent
Good Convertible Debentures	50 per cent	50 per cent	75 per cent
Listed Warrants	35 per cent	35 per cent	50 per cent
Puts and Calls	none	none	none
Commodities	85 per cent	. . . . . .	. . . . . .
Real Property	90 per cent	. . . . . .	100 per cent

It must be clearly understood that even though an investor can get as much as 95 per cent of the value of a Treasury obligation, the loan source doesn't have to give it to him. In other words, just because good listed bonds can command loans of eighty per cent of their value it is not necessarily true that the loan source will grant such a large percentage. This depends of course on many factors, including: (1) the loan source; (2) the money market conditions; and (3) the ability of the borrower to repay.

By now it has been demonstrated that people can improve their profit picture in the purchase of securities, commodities, real property and other equities if they borrow money. And now it is time to talk about how to borrow money properly and where to go for the funds.

· · · · 3 · · · ·

Sources of Leverage

Ideally, a leverage operator should maintain accounts in at least two commercial banks and two stockbrokerage houses. And very often he should cultivate a private source of loan funds that can be used in an emergency.

In this regard apocrypha has it that there was once an enterprising young speculator (married and with two children) who hungered to make a long-term capital gain in American Telephone and Telegraph stock. At the time he considered his maneuver, the stock was trading at $50. And like every sensible speculator, the young executive fixed a sell limit even before he actually purchased his shares. In this case he decided that if he were fortunate enough to buy Big Telephone at $50, he would willingly sell out at $58. But disregarding the minute amount of commissions, he realized that to swing the purchase of 200 shares of Ma Bell he would need at least $10,000. And he only had readily available cash of $3,500. His problem naturally was to make $3,500 do the work of $10,000.

How?

The Mother-in-Law Game

Regulation T of the Federal Reserve Board dictates that if this purchase occurred through an American stockbroker, the purchaser would have to pony up at least 65 per cent of the purchase price on the 200 shares or $6,500. And Regulation U of the Fed bars purchase of this nature through a national bank, unless the purchaser plunks down 65 per cent of the purchase price or $6,500. It would seem on the surface that to buy 200 T on margin at a broker or bank the enterprising young man would require at least $6,500 and he had only $3,500 to play with. But he also was an artful financial dodger who knew the rules—and who had a devoted mother-in-law as a private loan source. To this good woman did the young speculator approach and whisper, "Ma, I need $6,500 for a couple of weeks. Believe me, the money is safe—and I'll give it back to you then for sure."

Now no mother-in-law in her right mind—and alive—will simply hand over $6,500 without a whimper, so she counters, "What do you need the money for?" And the son-in-law whispers: "I am doing something for the children. But don't tell your daughter. It's a surprise."

Flattered that she has been taken into her son-in-law's confidence for her grandchildren's benefit, the accommodating "mom" disgorges the money. And now the son-in-law phones his broker and buys (for cash) 200 T @ $50. He goes to one of his banks and withdraws $3,500 (plus the commissions) and mails his broker a check in full (using the mother-in-law's money also) for the shares, with instructions to "transfer the shares in my name and mail them to me as fast as possible. Thank you."

A few weeks later the registered mail envelope containing the 200 shares of A.T.&T. arrives. The investor now hies himself over to his other bank and walks into a loan officer's sanctum.

"And what can we do for you today?" smiles the accommodating banker-on-the-way-up.

"I need a loan; for a special purpose," admits the enterprising investor. "And I have some rather good collateral to put up." With that he extracts his 200 shares and plunks them down on the banker's spotless desk.

Duly impressed, the loan officer examines the certificates to see if they are genuine and then sighs, "How much do you want?" The investor immediately retorts, "How much can I get?"

Smoothly the banker reveals that his institution will be happy to lend as much as 70 per cent of the market value of the shares—*if the money is not going to be used for the purpose of buying more stock*. He also points out that as a condition of making such a loan, the bank requires the borrower to sign a special form attesting that he will *not* use the funds from the loan to buy more stock of any kind.

Outwardly shocked, but inwardly elated, the investor admits, "Oh no. I would *never* buy any more stock. This money will *save* my life." In a way he isn't lying. His life at home will not be worth living if he doesn't pay his mother-in-law back!

Presto, the loan is granted. The investor, of course, is charged "going rates," but as will soon be seen, the cost is worth the risk. Meanwhile, he manfully returns the $6,500—and if he can manage it, busses his mother-in-law in the process. Seven months later he calls his second broker and sells the 200 T he has in hock at one of his banks for $58. Why didn't he sell the shares at the brokerage firm he bought them from in the first place? Notwithstanding other valid reasons, he has left the impression with the first broker that 200 T has been locked away forever in his "vault." But how did he do with the trade?

His 200-share purchase cost
$10,000+$88 in commissions=$10,088.00
His 200-share sale garnered
$11,600−$89.60−tax $10   = 11,500.40

Gross before interest charges .... $ 1,412.40
Interest charges @9%−7 mos 367.50
Net profit on leveraged deal .... $ 1,044.90

How does this—expressed in percentages—stack up against the cash buyer or NYSE margin buyer who may have done the same thing?

Cash Buyer

$$\frac{1,412}{10,088}=13.4 \text{ per cent profit}$$

NYSE Margin Buyer

$$\frac{1,412-105 \text{ interest}}{\$8,088}=16 \text{ per cent}$$

Mother-in-Law-Bank Margin

$$\frac{1,412-367.50 \text{ interest}}{\$3,088}=34 \text{ per cent!}$$

Obviously, in order to make money it has to earn the highest percentage profit possible in any alternative situation. In the example above, $10,000 worth of one of the "safest" stocks on the Big Board is involved. If the investor uses his own money (cash buyer) he winds up with a 13.4 per cent profit. If he uses the niggardly margin permitted under existing—and unrealistic—federal rules at brokerage houses or banks he winds up with 16 per cent, a 2.6 per cent inducement that hardly seems attractive enough to invite the filling out of the lengthy —and exceedingly fine print—hypothecation forms. But the *informed investor* finds sources of leverage—*entirely legal*—to increase his profits whenever he takes a risk.

Naturally, not everybody has an accommodating mother-in-law, but almost everybody of substance has enough friends and neighbors who just might be able to accommodate him for the few weeks time it takes to make a purchase, receive the actual shares and arrange for a "special purpose" loan at a neighborhood commercial bank. It must be clearly kept in mind, however, that the shares *must be purchased for cash first* and borrowed upon later. If the credit is sought at the time of purchase, all an investor can get is a measly 35 per cent loan on good stocks.

Special-Purpose Loans

Incidentally, commercial banks will readily lend money for special-purpose loans on unlisted or over-the-counter securities, if the securities have merit. For example, owners of stock in the St. Louis Cardinals can borrow to the hilt on their shares, because the ball club is a top performer. But we wouldn't be too certain about the chances of getting more than 50 per cent as a loan on the shares of the Padres. The amount commercial banks will lend on shares of listed and unlisted companies varies, of course, with the company and with the policy of the individual bank. In general, fully-paid-for shares of worthwhile companies can command anywhere from 50 to 75 per cent of the market value as collateral for special-purpose loans.

Foreign Leverage

Few people do as much traveling today as Americans. The fly-now-pay-later plans evidently have been highly successful, and if such arrangements could be made with the casino operators in Puerto Rico, the Bahamas and Curacao, their businesses might show swollen profits too. Regrettably, few people on a holiday ever give a thought to financial affairs except to frenetically try to find a *Wall Street Journal*, or *New York Times* to follow their holdings while on vacation.

But—if leverage-minded—it pays to court the good will of foreign brokers and banks. The nearest foreign money handlers outside of this country, of course, are the Canadian bankers and brokers.

Canada, a nation of some 15 million people, has just begun to grow. And in 1955 and 1956 it looked like most of the speculative money from the United States would wind up north of the border. But the enactment of the interest equalization tax and the efforts of the SEC to muzzle stock promoters evidently stifled much of this outgo. Of course, if the *Northern Miner* had been banned as financial pornography not fit to be sent through the mails, much of the interest in moose pasture and mines alike would have been effectively cut off.

In any event, there is absolutely nothing to stop any American from going to Toronto or Montreal (stay away from Vancouver) to open accounts with member firms of the Exchanges in those cities, or with banks. The leverage advantages, of course, are tremendous.

Stocks listed on the Toronto, Montreal, New York and American Exchanges trading over $1 are marginable at 50 per cent of market value. Investors must avoid, like the plague, offices of New York Stock Exchange members who maintain memberships in Canadian Exchanges; these offices located in Canada will not accommodate Americans seeking better leverage than is available south of New Jersey. In other words, if an American wanders errantly into the Toronto office of a firm that is a member of the NYSE, the Toronto Exchange and the Montreal Exchange, he cannot maintain an account on Canadian terms unless he is a *resident* or is working in Canada. Small firms like E. H. Pooler, J. H. Crang, etc. are more accommodating.

How safe is money left on account, or stocks left on account with a Canadian broker? If he is a member of the Toronto Exchange, the position is about as safe as with any member of the NASD—and with most members of the NYSE. The Ontario Securities Commission is as zealously watchful for defalcation and trouble as any regulatory agency in the United States. And rarely has any American lost money because his assets were left in safekeeping at a Canadian member firm.

Perhaps the most appealing aspect of doing business with Canadian brokers on a leverage basis is the *day trade.*

Day Trading

In New York, there is a looked-down-upon breed of trader who is not an Exchange member and who tries to scalp himself a living by going in-and-out of a stock on the same day. To do this, Exchange requirements are 25 per cent of the value of the shares involved in the day trades on deposit in the speculator's margin account at all times. But recently—and because stocks often swing as much as ten or fifteen per cent during the same session—the Exchange arbitrarily hiked the margin to 65 per cent, for day traders who are "active." Thus while the rule of 25 per cent deposit remains for an occasional day trade, most day traders are faced with a 65 per cent burden in their attempt to scalp quick profits.

In Canada, however, the day trader has a Valhalla, or maybe a Garden of Eden. He can enter a NYSE stock in the morning and if he gets out of it the same day (at a profit or loss) he keeps the profit or makes good the loss on the trade *without putting up a single cent of margin money.* Notice that we are not advocating the day trading of Canadian securities. We allude *only* to American issues. More prevalent than day trading, however, is the exciting business of free riding.

Free Riding

Getting something for nothing is a strategy avidly sought after for as long as the seekers of the perpetual motion machine have labored. Getting something for nothing in the stock market involves the ancient practice of free riding—buying stock and later selling it *without ever putting up a dime to pay for the shares.* Free riding is divided into two sectors: (1) new issues, and (2) draft kiting.

Whenever a new issue is brought to the market, its shares begin to trade several weeks before the physical paper is available for transfer. On August 15, 1968, the subordinated debentures of Glen Alden, which were created to form an exchange for Schenley shares, were listed for trading in the Bond Section of the New York Stock Exchange, but the actual delivery of the debenture certificates occurred on or about September 9th. The day they opened tor trading a young man in his junior year at an Eastern university, employed for the summer at a member firm in New York as an "over-the-counter" trader, decided to buy some of the bonds. The youth had worked for the past five summers and had a small stake in addition to savings as a result of generous Bar Mitzvah presents. Because he was over 21 he didn't consult his father. And because the newspaper announcement of the tender offer indi-

cated that these bonds were in $100 denomina-
tions, he decided to buy $5,000 face value when
the bonds began trading.

Precisely on August 15th the debentures
opened—and traded—at $68. Figuring quickly,
the young man reckoned that $5,000 face value
would be $3,400 plus a small amount in commis-
sions. And so he promptly went out on the wire
and bought "fifty bonds." Little did he realize
that in so doing he was buying $50,000 face
value, or $34,000 in bonds. But he soon learned
his error. He also learned that since the bonds
were trading on a when-issued basis and would
trade that way until August 31st, he could
resell them at *any* time in that interval for a
profit or loss without giving his broker a penny.

When he arrived home with his story, his
father offered to put up the difference to cover
the error if his son wanted to keep the bonds
a while. But the young man confidently said,
"Look. I'll take a chance and free ride them
for a while without any money." And he did.
On August 31st he disposed of them for $72,
or a profit of slightly less than $2,000—*with
no deposit at all.*

Of course, Americans who had Toronto accounts could have bought $1 million or more of
these debentures and sold them out any time
until mid-September without putting up a dime.
To make profits without putting up any of your
own money is surely the essence of getting rich
on other people's money.

Draft Delivery

Those speculators who decide to play with
Canadian oil and mining and industrial shares

at Toronto or Canadian brokers can have a free ride for several weeks because the normal clearance period is fourteen days. In that time —because the stocks gyrate so much—a fortune can be made or lost.

The second method of getting free rides in the stock market is the risky business of kiting drafts. An American investor opens a substantial cash account with a Canadian bank. He calls a New York broker and buys 1,000 shares of a stock on the NYSE selling at $50. At the same time he instructs the broker to send the shares "draft attached" to the Canadian bank against payment by that bank for his account.

This delivery process may take as long as 30 days. Meanwhile the stock fluctuates. Assume that a few days after purchase the stock shoots up to $55. The speculator phones another New York broker, or his own Canadian broker, and orders the shares sold at 55. He also instructs the selling broker to send the check for the sale of the shares to the speculator's Canadian bank account against delivery of the shares. Now he sits back and waits for the bank to "cross" the transaction. When the buying broker delivers the shares in question to the bank, the bank will pay the buying broker, turn the shares over to the selling broker and deposit the check to the customer's account. Offsetting the purchase price and the bank fee, the draft-kiter's account winds up with the profit—or loss.

Frankly, at this writing there is no clear-cut body of law that stops brokers or other kinds of stock market operators from kiting drafts. The basic theory behind each and every stock purchase involved in this kind of an operation is that the buyer fully intends to make payment when the shares are delivered to the bank or broker specified in the "draft attached" instructions. Before attempting any operations of this nature it would be wise to check out the legality of doing this as a private individual. Assuredly, as a broker, there is no question of the legality of ordering stock to be delivered to a paying source. But if there is a question of legality in operating as an individual investor in this manner, it is relatively simple to become a broker. And at the rate stock exchanges are blossoming out all over the world, it shouldn't be either too difficult or too expensive to become a member of the Tel-Aviv Exchange, the Zambia Stock Exchange, etc. In any event, for active traders who could benefit from leveraging operations, it just might pay to become a registered broker—and even a member of the National Association of Securities Dealers. You do not have to do business with the general public in order to take advantage of some of the benefits of being a registered broker-dealer in any state in the Union today. But if you do not want to undergo the goldfish-bowl type of operation currently demanded by the Securities and Exchange Commission, explore the advantages and disadvantages of buying and selling via draft delivery.

Foreign Accounts

In summary, to open a Canadian bank account or brokerage account the leverage-minded trader must deposit a significant amount of cash or securities—and leave a sizable balance always on account. Nothing impresses domestic bankers or foreign bankers as much as money. And the operator who walks into a foreign bank with $2,000 will find himself looked down upon. The larger the opening deposit, the more respect he receives—and the more service he can expect to get.

Another nearby haven for leverage-minded investors who are interested in free riding the market is the Bahamas.

First rule: Do not open *any* accounts with brokers in Nassau. Deal *only* with banks—preferably Barclay's Bank. Any substantial person can receive an entrée from his American banker friends to bankers in the Bahamas. This entrée, usually in letter form, opens the path to many things, including transmission of securities drafts. The Federal Reserve permits the payment of stock shipped by draft to lag for as much as 30 days. And in dynamite markets a free rider can find that a potential loss becomes a profit if he waits a bit before selling. This method gives him a decided edge over traders who deal with New York firms and are forced to sell out the same day that they purchase stock.

The best part of dealing in Nassau or in Canada is that there are no significant taxes against an investor's profits. But *Americans, of course, are compelled to declare and pay taxes on profits earned in the stock market whether the trades were settled in New York, Toronto, Nassau or Geneva.*

Speaking of the Swiss banks, sophisticated leverage tacticians have long ago learned one word: *avoid.* In the first place, merely the mention that an investor has a Swiss bank account alerts the Internal Revenue Bureau like the quarry's scent to a hound. The same may be true of Nassau dealings. In the second place, $15,000 or $50,000 is peanuts to the "gnomes." Moreover, funds deposited with Swiss banks for safekeeping are "invested." Although the safety of these funds depends upon the reputation of the bank, the charges for foreign leverage operations can give any investor a financial rupture.

The Borrowed Money Game

Before the arbitrary enactment of Regulation G of the Federal Reserve, which extended Fed. regulations on margin and credit to *unregulated* money lenders, several Swiss banks had New York offices that busily accommodated buyers and sellers of American securities according to Swiss rules.

In this regard, they extended loans running six months and longer at rates of one per cent a month on the amount borrowed—but *off the top*. In other words, if an investor seeking a leveraged long-term capital gain had bought 200 T at 50 and had held for 7 months to sell at 58, his situation would have looked something like this:

Purchase of 200T @50=10,088 (including commissions)
Sale at 58   =11,540 (after commissions)
   Gross profit before
     interest charges = 1,412.40
Loan of $7,500 for
   7 months, interest
   plus charges   =   587.50
Net profit   = $824.90

$$\text{Percentage on transaction}=\frac{824.90}{2,500}=33 \text{ per cent}$$

If the mother-in-law-levered hero earlier in this chapter had maneuvered his trade at a bank that would lend him 75¢ on every dollar of paid-for Telephone, but at reasonable rates, his profit would have been:

$$\frac{1,105.75}{2,500} = 44 \text{ per cent!}$$

That is why it is *cheaper* to cultivate one's mother-in-law than the little men of mystery who made Adam Smith's delightful essay a best-seller.

We freely admit ignorance of operations in Liechtenstein, France, Germany, Italy, Israel and points West. Beyond question, the best place in the world for leverage-minded traders and investors was Cuba. But with Cuba dead (how can it be alive under Communism?), the next best place is Canada.

The Loss Factor

Until this point we have perhaps emphatically stressed the profit power of leverage operations. It should always be remembered that the *chance for loss* increases directly with an increase in the amount borrowed. Thus, the buyer of Big Telephone for cash can salt it away for his heirs without a worry. The fellow who borrows at his broker does not have to be too concerned with how far down his stock goes before he will get a "margin call." The dichotomous faces of NYSE and Federal margins are that when initially a customer had to deposit 80 per cent of the value of the newly purchased listed shares, he was only compelled to maintain 25 per cent of the market value if the shares decline. Thus a purchaser of 200 T on 80% margin at $50 puts up $8,000. But how far down does Telephone have to go before he may be called for margin? At $25, the customer has obviously lost $5,000 of his equity (on paper) but the $3,000 equity remaining in his account is far more than the $1,250 required by Exchange maintenance margin regulations. What is the situation if T declines to $20? At that point the value of the 200 shares has dipped to $4,000; and the customer's equity has declined to $2,000—still *double* the protection the Exchange requires in its 25 per cent maintenance margin regulations.

The following table, predicated on the purchase of 100 shares of listed stock at $100 a share, indicates danger points on purchases according to varying degrees of Federal margins, ranging from 50 per cent to 80 per cent:

Stock Purchase $10,000, Stock Bought @100

Margin	*Must Decline to*
80 Per Cent	25
70	40
50	66 2/3

Unquestionably, the Exchange firms would send out margin calls before the stock dropped to the danger levels above. Whether or not they would be justified in "selling out" an account that didn't get up the money on a margin call above the requirement is a moot point, often argued at long length in the courts.

House Rules

Notice that when real leverage begins to rear

its head (50%), the $100 stock has to decline to about $67 before a New York broker will take action. The same is true with mother-in-law-bank-arranged special-purpose loans. In the case of securities held at Canadian banks, brokers or foreign banks, the rule of maintaining 25 per cent of the market is not adhered to. Often, however, these people can be extremely arbitrary about their "house regulations."

In 1956 an American speculator maintained a position of 200,000 shares of a Canadian stock trading at $1 40 a share at a member firm of the Toronto Exchange. The bundle was margined at 50 per cent in accordance with Exchange rules. But suddenly the managing partner of the firm got fidgety and decided he wanted "100 per cent, or get the account the hell out." The speculator couldn't raise the money and the shares were subsequently dumped on the market dropping the stock to 90 cents, at which point it became ineligible for margin and caused selling at other brokerage accounts that had margin privileges— with the result that eventually the beleaguered stock dropped to a nickel a share. It has since recovered to 15¢. But the point is that the abortive break in the stock would have never occurred if the Exchange member hadn't arbitrarily broken the price of the stock by declaring a change in his house margin rules.

In this regard something must be said about the arbitrary—and often hard to understand— attitude of the sanctimonious members of the New York Stock Exchange who brag about the kind of service they give investors. Many of them alter Exchange rules to suit their own desires and situations.

For example, in 1968, the paper blizzard that stopped up most back offices caused the Exchange to rule Wednesday closings. This deprived Americans of the right to buy or sell stock on Wednesdays unless they resorted to dealers outside the country or to NASD members. Moreover, some firms, like Paine, Webber, Jackson & Curtis, arbitrarily declared they wouldn't open margin accounts for customers with less than $5,000 in said accounts. The Exchange rule is a minimum of $2,000. In connection with over-the-counter stocks, many firms have ruled that they will not buy (for accounts of clients) stocks under $5 a share. Yet these very same firms may have been instrumental in floating issues that have declined from more than $5 a share to pennies. Thus if investors are stuck with over-the-counter paper losses in stocks that were sold to them by Exchange firms, they cannot readily double up to establish tax losses or to average unless they go elsewhere. In the light of these arbitrary practices, and knowing that the customers with big debit balances get a better rate of interest than the customers in the same firms with small debit balances, it just might behoove the small investor to avoid Exchange firms altogether. But enough of the gloomy side of the situation. What if an investor manages a highly leveraged position at a domestic or foreign bank or broker and the stock zooms? He now attains something of magic called "buying power"—and can pyramid by buying more shares with the additional equity created by the advance in his position.

To examine this power to buy more shares from the market increase of shares already existing in an investor's portfolio, it is fitting to digress for one chapter from the anecdotal style of this book and become a bit professorial.

····4····

The Power of Pyramiding

Every intelligent investor or trader seeks to put his capital to the most fruitful use. Business corporations employing leverage and utilizing their assets to maximize earnings generally are most successful in good times. To attain the greatest benefit from his risk endeavors in the market, a wise investor uses the *buying power* generated by the *paper appreciation* in his portfolio to buy more stock. Simply put, this is the process of pyramiding.

Assume that two investors are able to land a lucky position in 100 shares of stock at a source that is satisfied to carry the account on 50 per cent margin—with the client *always maintaining an equity in his account of 50 per cent of the market value of his position*. The purchase of 100 shares of stock at 40, financed in this manner, would look like this:

Number of Shares	Market Price	Value	Loan	Margin, or Deposit
100	$40	$4,000	$2,000	$2,000

Since at this point the customer's *equity* (assets minus liabilities) is the same as his margin or deposit, it will be called from now on the equity. Assume that the leverage buyer is fortunate and the stock soars after eight months — in 10-point-a-month intervals — to $120. This is how his position appears by the ninth month:

Month	Market Price	Market Value	Loan	Equity
January	$40	$4,000	$2,000	$2,000
February	50	5,000	2,000	3,000
March	60	6,000	2,000	4,000
April	70	7,000	2,000	5,000
May	80	8,000	2,000	6,000
June	90	9,000	2,000	7,000
July	100	10,000	2,000	8,000
August	110	11,000	2,000	9,000
September	120	12,000	2,000	10,000

On paper, therefore, this lucky investor indicates a possible profit of five times on his original $2,000 deposit. Assume that at the $120 level he envisions another 100 points on the upside for this wonder stock, and he is reluctant to add any funds from his cash reserves—how many shares can he buy of the same stock without putting up a penny?

Buying Power

Since the terms of this hypothetical margin situation are that he can buy stock on 50 per cent margin and the equity in the account must represent at least 50 per cent of the value of the account, he can buy another $8,000 worth, or 65 shares—without putting up a dime. In other words, his *buying power* under the terms of the loan agreement is $8,000 worth of the stock, because he has in his account at the 120 level an *excess* of $4,000 above the required equity of $6,000 needed at that price level.

Obviously, the increase in the paper value of the investor's shares could have been turned into real—and taxable—profits simply by liquidation at the $120 level, or at any level above $41 (figuring commissions). But a smart devotee of margin operations would never have sold. If he had, he would have been liable for taxes (from the 40 to the 120 level) on a long-term basis, and would have *missed the market* by selling too soon if the stock subsequently shot up to $200. Yet often profits are taken because of a need to generate cash. If this were the case with our lucky friend, he could have generated $4,000 in cash immediately at the $120 level by asking the broker or bank to give the *excess* in the form of a check or cash. How would the investor's account at $120 appear if he did this?

Market Price	Shares	Value	Loan	Equity
120	100	$12,000	$6,000	$6,000

Notice that by giving the investor a check for $4,000, the loan source has increased its claim to $6,000 from $2,000 and the investor's equity has been reduced from $10,000 to $6,000.

Generating Cash

But he has generated cash amounting to half his market profit (from 40 to 120, or 80 points on 100 shares) without taking in any partners (Mr. Nixon, Mr. Rockefeller and Mr. Lindsay, if the investor lives in New York State).

Informed—and experienced—operators with leverage realize that as soon as the stock in the aforegoing example moved from $40 to $50 they could have bought more shares with their *buying power.* And when the stock moved from $50 to $60, they could have bought more stock not only on the original one hundred share lot's appreciation, but also on the appreciation of the odd lot they picked up at the $50 level. And the same goes for the $70, $80 and other levels all the way up to the $120. Assume that a pyramiding expert decided to pyramid his position of 100 shares, margined precisely under the same circumstances as the cautious investor who margined one hundred shares and laid a big fat paper profit egg while it went up in price from $120—how would the account have fared?

Month	Market Price	Number of Shares	Value	Loan	Equity
January	$40	100	$4,000	$2,000	$2,000
February	50	120	6,000	3,000	3,000
March	60	140	8,400	4,200	4,200
April	70	160	11,200	5,600	5,600
May	80	180	14,400	7,200	7,200
June	90	200	18,000	9,000	9,000
July	100	220	22,000	11,000	11,000
August	110	240	26,400	13,200	13,200
September	120	260	31,200	15,600	15,600

Pyramid Power

A quick comparison shows the rather awesome power of pyramiding this way. Notice that at the 120 level the fully pyramided investor's equity is $15,600, whereas the cautious investor's equity at the same level is $10,000—a difference of some 56 per cent. Moreover, the rise to 120 in the second investor's fully margined portfolio was accomplished by the momentum created by a portfolio of 240 shares (the last 20 do not count unless the stock goes higher), whereas the paper profit of the first investor's position was generated on 100 shares.

Without counting commission costs or interest on the loans involved, the second investor theoretically has gained more than 7½ times his original, out-of-pocket outlay of $2,000, while the first investor has made five times his original $2,000 deposit.

For the more mathematically minded readers, my nephew, Jonathan Shane (MIT, 1968; MBA, 1970), has prepared the following formula which can pinpoint precisely how much equity and loan value would be evident in any position that increases in equal increments, where an original position of equity amounting to 50 per cent of the market value is maintained for a specific number of points of market rise broken down into equal increments:

$$E_i = L_i = \frac{P_i N_i}{2}$$

$$N_i = N_o\left(1 + \frac{i\Delta P}{P_o + \Delta P}\right) = N_o + \frac{N_o i\Delta P}{P_o + \Delta P}$$

$$P_i = P_o + i\Delta P$$

$$i + \frac{P_i - P_o}{\Delta P}.$$

Explanation of symbols:
L = loan
E = equity

$P = $ price increment
$N = N_{t+1} - N_t = $ additional stock purchased in a period
$N_o = $ original stock purchase
$P_o = $ original price
$P_i = $ price after increase in price of P.

Up to this point a theoretical—and admittedly ideal—situation has been put forth to explain the power of pyramiding. But in a lesser degree, any investor who owns fully-paid-for stock can generate buying power in the same, or other securities. For example, a person who has a cash account at any member firm of the New York Stock Exchange can switch his position to a margin account and generate security buying power.

Account Switching

Assume an account has $50,000 in fully-paid-for stocks listed on the Big Board, trading over $5 a share, and now switches his holdings to a margin account. How much buying power will he have on a margin basis? How much cash can he generate by doing this?

Current federal regulations permit listed securities of a national exchange to be carried by regulated banks and brokers at 65 per cent margin. So immediately the account generates a $17,500 loan from his broker. Since his new purchases will be carried at 65 per cent, the $17,500 will buy $26,900 worth of new securities. Here is how the new position would look:

Portfolio Value	Equity	Loan
$76,900	$50,000	$26,900

Dr. Leo Barnes has worked out an ingenious, but simple method of quickly calculating an account's position at any time:

CURRENT EQUITY = market value of portfolio — debit balance (loan).

EXCESS = current equity — required margin.

CASH WITHDRAWAL or C𝐴SH BUYING POWER = EXCESS.

BUYING POWER = Excess divided by margin requirement, in per cent.

Assume the same person with $50,000 worth of good, listed securities needed $25,000 for a worthwhile purpose. Chances are he could borrow at a commercial bank *at least* that amount in jig time. But, of course, he would have to sign a statement saying he does not intend to use the money generated by the loan to buy more stock.

Now if the person involved *does* want to buy stock and does not desire to violate federal regulations, or evade them through some ill-concealed artifice, he can be a legitimate artful dodger by taking his stocks to Canada. There he can immediately generate $25,000 in the form of a cash withdrawal loan—and his portfolio—if he instead buys more stock—will look like this:

Portfolio Value	Loan	Equity
$100,000	$50,000	$50,000

In other words, he can add $50,000 more of the *same* stocks, or any other quality issues, in Canada, while he is restricted to a purchase of only $26,900, in the United States.

So why don't more people do it?

The answer simply is they *do not know*, or else they would have carted their holdings north long ago. And remember: the ratio of what can be done with $50,000 can be done with $5,000. You do not have to be rich to make money on other people's money.

Leveraged Triple Play

In the days of my boyhood, people still remembered Tinkers to Evers to Chance—the triple-play boys. A devotee of leverage *pyramids* his holdings for all they are worth. And the rules bother him not a bit, because to get around them legally he dabbles in *two areas at once:* the stock market and real estate.

The third party in this triple play to make millions is the bank, spelled *b-a-n-k.*

The way this combination bit of pyramiding works is that the investor must begin with cash, say $100,000. He buys this much good stock and pays for it. He then withdraws his shares and brings them over to the bank, borrowing 70 per cent of market value in order to buy real estate.

His $100,000 stock position is protected by a $30,000 deposit. The $70,000 special-purpose loan now goes to buy a piece of income-producing property for $280,000. A bit of ingenuity on the part of the real estate investor and the rents are hiked. On this basis, the mortgage on the property can be increased to $280,000 from its present mortgage of $210,000. The operator now creams off his original $70,000 and goes back in the market to buy $70,000 worth of stock which he can take to another bank and hock for 70 per cent of the value, or $49,000. With the roughly 50 grand he gets from the bank he can look for another building, garage, etc. And so it goes, from broker to banker to Realtor and back.

And, of course, if necessary there are always second mortgages. In any event, a smart operator using latter-day Tinkers to Evers to Chance can make a million fast—without breaking the leverage rules—if he is nimble, if his stocks stay up and if he can successfully "mortgage himself out" of good realty situations.

What happens to pyramiders when the market suddenly goes into a sharp—and prolonged —decline? My friend Nicolas Darvas echoes market advice that came with the *Mayflower:* "Run like a thief."

Maybe he's right. No one ever got killed taking small profits—especially people who play with leverage.

Leveraged Prudence

But because the leveraged operator is exposed to greater risks than the cash buyer, it is obvious that he must move faster to shift his holdings when trouble approaches. Many years back I knew a trader who liked American Motors. He bought it at 26, bought more at 32, more at 43, more at 46, more at 60 and kept buying all the way up to 85. By what instinct of self-preservation he decided to liquidate near the top of this stock's meteoric rise I will never know, because my friend has been buried long ago from angina pectoris; but obviously he decided he had pyramided far enough and so he went—before the bottom fell out of AMC after its split. The point being that prudent pyramiders—if there is such an obviously anachronistic category—make their switches sufficiently in advance of price reversals to save their skins. If they don't or are stubborn about a losing stock's chances of coming back, they wind up in bankruptcy courts or in the cemetery from heart attacks. After all, an investment decision should be based on more than gossip in a dentist's office. And wise pyramiders have their investment ears tuned to the scene almost 24 hours a day. They realize there is a time to get out of cyclical stocks and into defensive issues, or out of war stocks into peace stocks, etc. Perhaps Baruch's pilfered advice "cut losses and let profits run" is more appropriate to pyramiders' positions than any single piece of Wall Street's multitude of platitudes.

And now for commodities, an area that is occult, but shouldn't be, for most speculators. In no area of the market are opportunities to make killings by *pyramiding* or otherwise as prevalent as they are in commodities.

···· 5 ····

Commodities — and
Personal Leverage

For some as yet unexplained reason, the
rules of the New York Stock Exchange
permit its members to grant reasonable
leverage terms of purchase on some of
the most speculative items known to
man: commodities futures. Here, speculators are accepted as a necessary part of
the process known as hedging (in the
professional sense) by growers and producers and actual users of the commodities involved. The speculator is needed,
of course, to "provide liquidity" to the
marketplace. In other words, what the
brochures so artfully hide is that the
speculator is needed to be one side of a
professional's two-sided hedging operation.

The Hedging Habit

By professionals we do not allude to brokers or dealers or investment managers as we do when speaking of the stock market. Rather we mean the people directly affected by the commodities in question as part of their regular business. To explain: a city-based baker knows he cannot pay more for flour at any time in order to sell his bread to the supermarkets at a set price and still come out alive with a profit. In January, he, of course, cannot tell what he will have to pay for flour in May. To protect his May output he buys May wheat futures in January and is "hedged." In other words, if the price of wheat declines in the interim, he is going to use the wheat for flour anyway. And if it rises, he is protected by his forward purchase. For the professional user, the commodities markets and futures trading are a *necessary* way of life. Because of this, and because of regular usage by growers, producers, grain elevator operators, metal manufacturers, etc., alert speculators (a nice word in the commodities arena) can glean enormous (percentagewise) profits on very little outlay. But before entertaining strategies to make market killings in commodities on a "shoestring" it is fitting to dwell a bit on hedging.

By definition hedging is a technique in the commodities markets for insuring future output against price changes. It enables the merchant or manufacturer or farmer to protect his merchandise against more than minor price changes by passing the risk on to speculators who habitually deal in futures. Moreover, it is easy for the professional to borrow money against hedged inventories. Thus spinners and mills hedge in cotton futures. Soap manufacturers hedge in lard, etc. In 1966, Wilson & Co. expanded a plan whereby it contracts for hogs on a future-delivery basis and hedges the contract through a sale of hog futures.

Assume hogs are selling in the future market at $21 and the cost of delivering them to the Cedar Rapids, Iowa, plant of Wilson is $1.50, a hog producer will net $19.50 a hundred in April if he signs a contract with Wilson in September to deliver said hogs at that price.

Meanwhile, and simultaneous with its signing of the contract with the hog producer, Wilson sells off its buy contract. When the hogs are delivered in April, Wilson buys the contract back. The company stands to neither profit nor lose on its transactions, but it does *assure* the hog producer of the going contract price. In this manner the hog raisers are benefitted and the packing company has an assured source of raw materials to process.

Those Active Commodities

Here is a listing of active commodities that are currently traded in the futures markets, together with contract terms, round-turn commission rates, etc.:

Commodity	Initial Mgn.	Contract Size	Round-Trip Chgs*	Close-to-Close Daily Limits
LIVE CATTLE	$ 500	25,000 lbs.	$36	1½¢/lb.
COCOA	$1,000	30,000 lbs.	$40 to $60	1¢/lb.
COFFEE	$1,200	32,500 lbs.	$50 to $80	2¢/lb.

EGGS (Chi.)	$ 500	15,000 dz.	$36	2¢/dz.

Controlled Commodities

COTTON (N.Y.)	$ 500	50,000 lbs. (100 bales)	$45	2¢/lb.
CORN	$ 600	5,000 bu.	$22	8¢/bu.
OATS	$ 350	5,000 bu.	$18	6¢/bu.
RYE	$ 900	5,000 bu.	$22	10¢/bu.
SOYBEANS	$2,000	5,000 bu.	$24	10¢/bu.
WHEAT (Chi.)	$ 900	5,000 bu.	$22	10¢/bu.

Metals

COPPER	$1,500	50,000 lbs.	$51.50	2¢/lb.
LEAD	$ 500	60,000 lbs.	$51.50	1½¢/lb.
ZINC	$ 500	60,000 lbs.	$51.50	1¢/lb.

Misc.

POTATOES (Maine)	$ 200– 400	50,000 lbs.	$23	35¢/100 lbs.
PORK BELLIES	$1,000	30,000 lbs.	$36	1½¢/lb.
HIDES	$1,000	40,000 lbs.	$41.50	2¢/lb.
RUBBER	$ 400	22,400 lbs.	$41.50	2¢/lb.
SUGAR (7 & 8)	$ 750	112,000 lbs.	$20 to $60	½¢/lb.

*Note: And size of contracts may change. Special rates for day trades and for straddles and spreads.

Note that in the list above there are two kinds of commodities: controlled and free. The controlled commodities are supervised by government agencies and are therefore less likely to fluctuate up or down. The exception, of course, is "beans" (soybeans).

A Market of Price Patterns

Notice that initial margin to control one contract of beans is $2,000, while to control a similar quantity of corn (5,000 bushels) only $600 is needed. If the market rose 8¢ on a corn contract, the holder on paper would have made a potential profit of $400 (before commissions) on his $600 deposit. If a contract of beans moved up the daily limit of 10¢, its owner would be ahead on paper $500 against his deposit of $2,000. The reason the brokers insist on three times as much deposit for a contract of beans as they do for corn is almost obvious. The beans move up and down about three times as fast.

Because of professional intervention in futures markets they are prone to follow preset patterns. Thus for thirteen years prior to 1954, September egg futures rose in price from January to April and then receded from April to September. In the winter of 1953 I became rather interested in these speculations, especially since a deposit of $750 controlled the movement of 14,400 dozen eggs. And so in January, 1954, I began to buy egg futures. So did my customers, family and close friends. From a beginning of less than 42¢ a dozen the price slowly climbed—as per the charts—to 48¢, to 50¢, to 52¢, to 54¢. And naturally, we pressed the issue, buying more. Luckily, as the price moved up, and as we pyramided, we entered stop-loss orders to sell, several cents under the purchase price of each contract.

Suddenly—and well in advance of the time the eggs were supposed to fall—they went down. One by one the stops went off, the contracts were sold and we got out with our skins. One intransigent customer, however, refused to put in a stop and stubbornly refused to sell out as the price fell. Down, down it went. By September it had hit an almost all-time low (within human memory) of 18¢ a dozen. This represented a $3,900 loss to the lone owner of

September eggs and he asked quaveringly if he could take delivery of the eggs themselves. I asked why and he answered, "Eggs are 50¢ a dozen in the store. I'll sell several dozen at 45¢ to your wife. Some more to your mother. Some more to your mother-in-law. And to your brothers, and cousins, and uncles, and aunts. I'll sell the whole 14,400 dozen at a sensible price, but I'm never going to sell the eggs for 18¢ a dozen to anybody."

After I explained that these weren't eggs nestled in boxes of one dozen each, he asked if he could take possession and store them until better prices appeared. To his credit, he did this. How much he eventually lost was never revealed, but he never sold them to anybody for 18¢—that's for sure.

Not so oddly, it later turned out that the egg market had been manipulated by a group of Chicago people who drove the price down on the short side and made a cleanup. Discounting the rare exceptions, however, commodities will move up or down practically faithful to price ranges of previous years. Interested speculators are therefore urged to deal with a large NYSE member firm that retains memberships, has a commodities department and issues regular bulletins. In New York and Chicago there are several small firms, like Kroll, Dallon, members of commodities exchanges, who perform management and advisory services for interested speculators. But as in other areas of the market, the wisest speculator takes his risks by calling the shots himself. After all if the people managing the speculations were certain of their actions they would be playing the market themselves, without being annoyed by disgruntled speculators who run to the SEC when they lose.

Inflation Factor

Those of us who have lived from World War I through President Johnson's expensive administration have lived to see prices of almost everything shoot up beyond belief. It was not too long ago (1939) that I was able to buy two packs of Luckies for a quarter. Now I'm fortunate if I get a nickel change from a dollar for the same two packs. Thus instead of eight packages of cigarettes for a dollar we now get about two. This should do as much to end smoking as the fancy TV advertisements reflecting the symbol of the American Cancer Society. But while in almost every area of endeavor prices have zoomed appreciably since World War II, *the prices of commodities have not.*

This amazing refusal to rise has been attributed to government intervention. But how long this will remain—especially with a new helmsman in Washington—is debatable. Professor A. Zelomek of the University of West Virginia, one of America's best known but least publicized economic forecasters, predicts that the prices of commodities *must* rise in the near future. The world starvation situation, the increasing costs of production on the farm and processing in the food plants predicate such a rise. Now wouldn't it be just fine to be sitting in January on 10 contracts of September eggs purchased at 30 cents a dozen and watch them climb the 2¢ a dozen daily limit by Easter time to 60¢? In that happy event, the speculator would sell out for a gross profit per contract of $4,500 on his $500 deposit per contract—or 900 per cent on money? Or $45,000 on $5,000 deposit.

The best part about the whole thing, of course, is that when the speculator contracts to buy 15,000 dozen eggs at 30¢ a dozen which haven't even been laid yet, he does *not have to pay any interest whatsoever* on the balance of the price of the $4,500 contract that hangs above his deposit of $500. Because forward commodities are *futures*, no interest is ever involved.

Most of the money made by speculators in commodities, however, is not done by hedging, straddling or sitting with a bunch of contracts at one price and waiting for them to appreciate to some predetermined—and to-be-hoped-for—position. The money is made by pyramiding.

Pyramiding Media

Commodities are far superior to stocks as media for pyramiding purposes, the reason being that the *speculator has to protect the broker merely with a deposit rather than a fixed percentage of the market value of the futures.* In other words, if a speculator were to buy a contract of September eggs in January at 30¢ he has to deposit $500 "margin." The value of this $4,500 contract now begins to rise. Eggs stand in April at 60¢, making the 15,000 dozen contract worth $9,000. If the speculator liquidates he makes a gross profit of $4,500 on his deposit of $500, or nine times on his money. But let us assume that on February 1 the eggs were 40¢; March 1, 50¢ and April 1, 60¢; and that the investor-speculator had pyramided into more egg contracts of the' same month with his *buying power* at every 10¢ rise in price. This is how he would stand:

Market Price	# Contracts	Cash or Market-Generated Deposit	Paper Profit
30 cents	1	$ 500	$ 0
40	4	2,000	1,500
50	16	8,000	7,500
60	48	24,000	23,500

At this point the successful speculator can do a lot of things, including selling out and going short, or selling off a fractional part of his contracts, or at the 50-cent level simply not buy any more. In any event, if he bails out at the 60¢ level without pyramiding 32 more egg contracts to make a total of 48, he will get about $23,500 profit on his risk of $500. Compare this possible gain of 47 times on out-of-pocket money with the niggardly return possible through leveraging a $500 transaction in listed stocks —or the only 9 times profit on the $500 deposit had the speculator purchased merely one contract at 30¢ and sold out at 60¢. Moreover, these pyramiding transactions do not have to occur in Toronto, Paris or Basle. They can be done in any city, village and hamlet in the country through virtually any New York Stock Exchange member.

Not so oddly, commodity specialists who are expert in a specific area of trading will be found in and around the centers where such trading takes place. Prospective speculators in wheat and barley, for example, might seek out the counsel and services of commodity firms in Minneapolis. Others interested in soybeans would be wise to look up firms in the Chicago area specializing in "beans." In New York City, certain firms like Bache & Company excel in trading potato futures. And so it goes.

Commodity Specialists

In the event the prospective commodity speculator isn't sure, or doesn't want to go through the trouble of digging up—and making the acquaintance of—specialist commodity traders who maintain seats on commodity exchanges to service their own needs and the needs of a select clientele, perhaps it is best to seek out and cultivate a commodity specialist in the area of interest who operates for the large Exchange wire houses. New York Stock Exchange firms which specialize in virtually every area of commodities are:

Bache & Co., Inc.
E. F. Hutton
Paine, Webber, Jackson & Curtis
Merrill, Lynch, Pierce, Fenner & Smith, Inc.
Walston & Co., Inc.

In these giant wire houses with hundreds of branches from New York to Honolulu and overseas, there are skilled, competent service personnel to execute commodity orders anywhere and in any market. It pays to do business with experts.

Special Margin Dispensations

There are special margin dispensations for people who file letters with brokerage firms attesting that they are buying or selling futures as hedges for their regular business. In this connection, no margin at all is required. Some students of charts play with straddles and spreads in commodities in an attempt to profit from changes in the spread between the commodity bought and the commodity sold, or if it is in the same commodity, but different months, then the speculator seeks changes in the difference between the present price and the price as the futures approach the end of their terms.

For example, a speculator might sell coffee and buy cocoa futures of a specific forward month. Both futures thereafter might move in the same direction, but the spread (difference between the buy and sell prices at the time of making the contracts) might narrow or widen. In this event, the speculator could wind up with a profit. Of course if coffee shoots up in price and cocoa drops down, the speculator will suffer loss. Some speculators buy the futures of one month and sell the futures of another month in the same commodity. Here, if the spread changes, no matter which way the market goes they will wind up with a profit, albeit a small one. Marginwise, in such hedging or straddling transactions, the speculator puts up a pittance of the value involved in his hedged contracts.

Because commodities transactions depend upon a dichotomous market involving protection-seeking professionals pitted against profit-oriented speculators, any person desiring to enter this exciting arena should prepare himself thoroughly in advance by reading, listening—and learning. It makes sense to seek out beforehand qualified representatives of brokerage firms experienced in commodity futures trading. Regrettably—and despite the penchant of publishers to flood the market with "how to" books —the literature on this subject either deals mainly with the history of commodity trading, explanations of commodity exchange operations or both. Very little has ever been written by working professionals to help the hungry speculators seeking leveraged profits in this market.

History indicates that the people who manage to make the real killings in commodities didn't learn their success in books. They had to undergo long apprenticeships and often the ardors and anguish of severe losses before they became successful. A case in point was Arthur Cutten.

The Cutten Case

In 1890, as a young man of twenty, Arthur Cutten came off the farm in Guelph, Ontario, and traveled to Chicago to seek his fortune. For five years he slaved as a clerk in the shadow of the wheat pit at $4 a week. Somehow he managed to amass a bankroll of $1,000. By then he also knew *everything* there was to know about trading in futures. By successful pyramiding, it wasn't too long before Cutten was worth more than $5 million. And from 1926 through the Depression he paid the highest taxes of any individual residing in the Chicago area, including the Fields and the Armours.

Most of it came from speculation in futures—but Cutten *learned* the business before he plunged. "Who is wise?" a sage once asked. And the answer came, "He who learns."

Naturally, there is no assurance that knowledge alone will bring profits in any area of fluctuating prices; but chances are a knowledgeable person in commodities will fare better than one who "knows" the stock market.

Notice that in this book's chart of popularly traded futures the first item mentioned is "Live Cattle." For most neophytes dabbling in this kind of future is highly risky. But there are opportunities in cattle that present interesting leverage return, not only on an investor's own capital but also on other people's money.

···· 6 ····

Cow Deals

In olden—and perhaps golden—times, the cattle kings of Texas put some bulls and cows out on the open range and let nature do its duty to make them rich. At every roundup the herd increased, the calves were branded and eventually the longhorns were driven off to market along the old Chisholm Trail. But progress impinged upon the bailiwick of the cattle barons, and the homesteaders fenced off the range.

Thereafter, a new bioscience involving animal husbandry and breeding arose. The longhorns went the way of automobile running boards as the Herefords and the Black Angus steaks-on-the-hoof took over. Meanwhile, the open range was put to much more profitable use by golf course and real estate developers. Still the cattle had to be sustained until sent to slaughter. And so there arose in these United States a breed of professional "feeders."

Feed-Lot Fortunes

These are animal dieticians who can take calves and confine them to a small area, "feeding pens," and feed the young animals scientifically so that when grown full size the beef-on-the-hoof will be sent to market and command better prices than those cattle that still graze on whatever range is left to the giant ranches. Because of the operations of the scientific cattle feeders a unique leverage situation exists.

Feeders operate in several ways: (1) they take all the risk themselves and keep all the profits after expenses; and (2) they let the investing public in on a good thing for part of the profits.

Of course, operations of a feeder who selfishly retains all the fruits of his own knowledge, banking connections and husbandry efforts would not interest potential speculators as much as some of the more cooperative efforts of cattle feeders that could bring qualified investors profits—without ever putting up a cent!

A Typical Cow Club

A feeder forms a cow club of speculators or investors who file financial statements with a specific bank. The club, using the services of the bank, opens an account with said bank in which the bank deposits money that has been borrowed by each individual club member on the basis of his financial statement. The money is used to buy calves which are boarded with the feeder. After 200 days, the calves are full-grown steers and are shipped to slaughter. The bank, acting as the seller of the beef, collects the money from the sale, deducts costs of feeding, insurance, transportation, interest, etc. and credits the club account with the profits. The account is then dissolved and another club formed. In the meantime the members of the cow club have achieved profits for the 200 days, running from 3 to 27 per cent on the amount of the loan debited to their individual share of the entire club account at the bank.

The beautiful part of this operation is that the members of the cow club do not use a single cent of their own money. To own a share in the club according to their financial status, the members use bank money for the entire operation from start to finish.

So if this scheme is so good, why doesn't everybody do it?

In the first place, most people who might qualify as members of such exclusive financial clubs do not know of their existence. In the second place, there are only a limited number of club openings available at any one time. In the third place, the number of banks that enter into such an operation are few and far between. But assuredly to earn money on the basis of one's financial reputation without putting up any "seed money" as a good-will deposit is really the summit of trying to get rich with other people's money.

So where does one find out about cow clubs and cow feeding plans?

Kansas City banks are active in financing

feeders. So are state banks in Illinois. The information used in this book came from a bank in East Urbana, Illinois. But banks in any rural area that make loans to scientific feeders might either form club accounts or arrange to have the person with money make investments jointly with the feeder involved.

So go to Kansas City or East Urbana and stop in at the nearest bank specializing in feeder loans. Get friendly with the bank president. Before you know it you too may be feeding cattle with bank money—that is if you as an applicant can plunk down a financial statement that would permit a bank to extend a $35,000 to $50,000 line of cattle feeding credit on the strength of your statement.

Stock Split in Beef

A handful of years back the wonder of the advertising world, Marion Harper (McCann-Erickson), startled the world of Wall Street when he flashed full-page ads in the *Wall Street Journal* announcing the sale of cattle of the Black Angus variety to people who were in the 90 per cent bracket and who were seeking capital gains. Buy a thing that splits its stock 100 per cent every year, he counseled. Knowing the mania of investors to seek long-term gains from stocks that split, Mr. Harper aroused their interest by displaying one Black Angus cow that became a cow and a calf after nature had worked its will. The essence of his plan was that investors would invest in a herd of their own which would be tended on a Harper enterprise and raised there. For three to five years the owner of the herd had to lose money, which, of course, he could take as a tax deduction. Later, he could sell the herd for a capital gain. Since the owner presumably was in the 90 per cent bracket, deductions from his income would cost the government 90 cents on the dollar. But on profits, the government would only get 25¢ on the dollar. Changes in the level down to 50 per cent as a maximum tax on personal income made this plan less attractive.

Evidently, the people who promote plans of this nature never give up. In the *New York Times* of Sunday, November 16, 1969, a huge ad depicting a pastoral scene of Black Angus cows filling their innards in the sunshine told one and all:

> If you are an investor in a high tax bracket—investigate the advantages of owning your own herd of purebred Aberdeen Angus cattle....

In the fine print at the top of the advertisement were the words: "This is neither an offer to sell nor the solicitation of an offer to buy these herds. The offering is made only by the Prospectus...." And offerings, dear readers, were in amounts of $100,000 as a "minimum participation."

What is most intriguing about this situation is that *not much cash* has to be laid out by the participant! For $100,000 he buys a one-third interest in a registered Aberdeen Angus breeding bull and 36 registered Aberdeen Angus females. This $100,000 purchase may be financed through promissory notes maturing in 52 months—and bearing simple interest of

7½ per cent a year—and this at a time when the prime rate (the very best rate to the most worthwhile borrowers at banks) was 8½ per cent. Meanwhile—as the purchaser watches his 36 females double due to the efforts of his one-third of a bull—all expenses incurred for herd depreciation, financing and maintenance charges and costs are completely deductible for federal income tax purposes. When the herd (the assets) is eventually sold, of course, the capital gains "thing" comes into play. And so here—for well-heeled investors who can command credit in blocks of $100,000 and can afford annual interest, maintenance charges, etc. while awaiting their bull-cow Eldorado—is the perfect investment. For years, while the herd is growing the investor gets tax deductions, and gives back to Uncle Sam a mere sliver of the eventual gains. The prospectus can be obtained from the Black Watch Herds Corporation, Fishkill Plains, Wappingers Falls, N.Y. 12590. But remember—you send for it at your own risk.

Banking Help

Wealthy people in the 50 per cent bracket can generally hire their own tax consultants and advisors. Raising cattle, sheep, hogs, chinchillas or any other form of salable life involves more than mere money. To be successful in these areas it takes much more than financing of the "inventory." And so unless the investor is lucky enough to have the status that will enable him to join a feeding club operated on bank money and by expert, scientific feeders, he should avoid the entire thing altogether. But if he does hanker to become a cattle breeder by using part of his own money and hocking his herd, he should seek out the best sources of advice, hire qualified people—and bank in Kansas City or in Illinois.

Personally, I have never liked the idea of becoming involved in an operation I know nothing about and where I have to depend almost entirely on the judgment and actions of others. If I were contemplating entering the cattle-raising business, I think I'd do some serious studying well in advance of taking any risks.

In previous chapters mention was made that New York Stock Exchange firms faithfully followed the initial margin requirements of the Federal Reserve Regulation T, which at this writing stands at 65 per cent of the market value of new stock purchased, providing said stock is eligible for margin under federal rules (listed on a national exchange and selling over $5 a share). But there are *exceptions* when New York Stock Exchange firms will carry purchases of such stocks—and even purchases of over-the-counter stocks—for as little as 25¢ on the dollar of the market value of the stock purchased. These exceptions are *special subscription accounts* and *conversions*.

7

Conversion Power

In the past twenty years, margin regulations monitored by the Federal Reserve Board have fluctuated between 50 and 80 per cent of the market value of new shares purchased. But not so oddly all that time—and including today too—there were opportunities for stock buyers to position stock requiring 65 per cent margin by only putting up 25 to 30 per cent of the value of the purchased shares. How? By carrying the shares in a special subscription account.

Listed Leverage

Such accounts are created whenever a company whose shares are listed for trading on the Big Board issues rights to its shareholders to subscribe to more stock during campaigns to raise capital. In this regard, of course, not every shareholder exercises his preemptive right by using the rights he receives to actually subscribe for the new shares of stock; but instead he will sell them for value.

The Exchange has ruled that if investors buy said rights and actually subscribe to the new shares, these shares can be carried with a deposit of 25 per cent of the value rather than with 65 per cent of the value as an initial deposit. Of course the rights which are purchased must be paid for, so the investor's eventual outlay will become about 30 per cent instead of 25. Obviously, if a person held 100 shares of XYZ trading at 100, and XYZ issued rights to subscribe for new shares at $90 to stockholders on the basis of one share of the new stock at the discounted price to every ten shares of stock already owned by the shareholder, his rights would have value. *But he could also sell out his stock; buy rights; pick up 400 shares of new stock from the treasury and carry them in a special subscription account.*

Shareholders who may be carrying long-term holdings on a 50 per cent margin basis can in the above situation sell out and replace their position in the *same* stock with twice as many shares.

Why doesn't everybody do it? Again, most investors are ignorant of the workings of a special subscription account. Second, only listed stocks that issue rights can be subscribed for by investors and carried on a 25 per cent basis. Third, increase of shares under this method increases the brokerage loan and increases the danger of being sold out in a down market. Finally, the Exchange requires that stock pur- chased on subscription *must be brought up to the full 65 per cent margin requirement in four equal quarterly payments.* So the seeker of high leverage in this manner must be careful to either have more money ready to put into the account, or take the risk of selling out at some time during the first three months after his account has been opened.

The advantages to people who already own stock for cash in an issue that is undergoing a subscription campaign are immediately obvi- ous. Assume that a stockholder owns 100 XYZ at $100, the market price. The issue is under- going a subscription at $90 according to already stated terms of ownership. He sells out at $100 and subscribes to 400 shares. Three months later, the stock is $150. How many shares does he have to sell off to own the balance free and clear?

At time of subscription the account appears:

Price	# Shs.	Loan	Equity	Cost of Rights
$90	400	$27,000	$9,000	$4,000

After three months with market value $150 a share:

Price	# Shs.	Value	Loan	Equity
$150	400	$60,000	$27,000	$33,000

Obviously he could liquidate the subscription account at this time, keep at least 200 shares (value $30,000) fully paid for and pocket the difference for cigars and a few Broadway shows. By doing this, the leverage-minded stockholder winds up with 200 shares of the company instead of 100. What happens, however, if the price of the stock had declined to $75 a share? The owner of 400 shares on subscription would have had to see his mother-in-law, or sell something else, to preserve his position by putting up the extra maintenance margin his broker would have insisted upon. The main discouraging fact about operating subscription accounts is that *as soon as the price of the stock which is subscribed for begins to decline* the stockbrokerage firm maintaining the account will call for more margin (additional cash). How much more? It depends on the firm involved. Wall Street firms were never kind to the little guys—and they certainly are not at this writing either.

But a smart investor who is well-schooled in the occult art of stock market leverage, doesn't have to wait for subscriptions in order to buy stock for three months on 25–30 per cent margin. He can do so all year round, on *any* stock over $5 a share listed on the big board, Amex, or traded over-the-counter through the expert use of puts and calls. To understand how this is accomplished—the purchase of securities on 25 per cent margin when uninformed investors must abide by the 65 per cent Regulation T rule, and accomplish this without violating said rule—the investor must know something more than merely a passable amount about *conversions*.

Conversion Power

Most investors are familiar with the fact that in Wall Street the legal definition of "conversion" is the process of exchanging one security for another—i.e., a bond for shares of stock; a warrant into shares of stock; rights into shares of stock; etc. The illegal concept of conversion is the changing of a customer's securities into cash and the misuse of said cash by the broker. But we are here not concerned with illegality.

The more sophisticated devotees of the ticker tape are quite aware that put-and-call dealers can change (convert) a put to a call and a call to a put at will, by using New York Stock Exchange firm trading accounts as accommodating "bankers."

To illustrate: a put-and-call dealer buys a put contract on 100 XYZ at $100 for six months and pays the option seller a fee of $600 for the item. At the same time, the put-and-call dealer *really* needs a call on XYZ at $100 which he has already promised to a call buyer. To create the call from the put he has purchased, the dealer calls a conversion house (NYSE firm that accommodates put-and-call dealers) and asks the firm to buy 100 XYZ at $100 in its own trading account (no commissions). The NYSE firm obliges and the put-and-call dealer gives said firm the put he has purchased for protection, while the conversion house *sells* a call on the stock it has purchased. In this manner, the conversion house cannot lose any money on the downside by virtue of its protective put, nor can it make any money on the upside, because the shares in its trading account have now been locked up against the outstanding call. So how does the conversion house make money? Well, it charges a fee for the call it sells to the dealer. This fee includes double floor brokerage, transfer tax and an interest charge based on the going market for "conversion money."

Meanwhile, the NYSE firm will hock the shares it has purchased and protected by a put for 90 cents on the dollar with appropriate bankers, and make an overage on the interest differential between what it pays the bank and what it charges the dealer. The put-and-call dealer, of course, will add on something to these charges and will figure it into the cost of the newly created call. So when the dealer buys a put on XYZ at $100 and pays $600 to the seller for the put—and converts it with a conversion house—the newly created call will cost him all told as follows:

1. Cost of put $600.00
2. Six-month conversion (rates at time this book is being written) 476.25
3. Charges from the conversion house for floor brokerage, etc. in round figures 16.00
4. Total cost $1,092.25

Chances are the put-and-call dealer will resell this call which has been created from a put for roughly $1,150 (plus transfer tax: all calls carry taxes—none for puts).

So what has all this to do with the fellow who wants to carry a listed or unlisted position on 30 per cent margin while the rest of the world has to pay 65 per cent? It has *plenty* to do with it. In fact, the dealer's ability to change puts into calls and calls into puts has created a wonderfully legal loophole for avid speculators who hunger to take the risks of ownership with other people's money. And it works like this.

Sell a Put: Buy a Call

Instead of an investor going long (buying) 100 shares of a stock, he sells (the professional lingo is "writes") a put on the stock, sells it to a dealer who converts the put into a call at a conversion house and then sells the investor back the newly created call. What has happened? By virtue of his having sold the put he has made a future possible purchase if the stock goes down; and by virtue of having bought the call, he has of course created control over the 100 shares of stock the conversion house purchased if the price of the stock moves up.

In other words, when he completes both sides of this transaction (sells the put and buys the call) he does not *own* any shares physically, but he holds *contracts* that *assure* him of ownership no matter which way the market goes! How does this create leverage?

New York Stock Exchange minimum margins for the sale of puts against a cash deposit are 25 per cent of the value of the shares of the stock involved. And the costs of conversion for the six months would run about six per cent or one per cent a month figuring all other charges. So, conceivably, the conversion-minded investor can create an ownership position in

XYZ with as little as $2,500 margin at his broker and an out-of-pocket $550 expended for the creation of his call. Why $550? Because, referring to the previous example, the put-and-call dealer *pays* the investor $600 for taking the risk of creating the put (*see* line 1). So the out-of-pocket money for the investor here is a total of $1,092.25 (line 4) from which is subtracted the $600 put premium paid by the dealer (line 1) leaving the cost of the call actually $492.25 + $57.75 (dealer's profit), or a total of $550.

In effect, therefore, the investor simulates a long position on 100 XYZ trading at $100 a share for the next six months, while he only puts up the sum of $3,050 instead of the required $8,000 to buy the *same* stock under existing margin regulations. Notice that at this writing more than 100 issues have been relegated to the 100 per cent margin category by the Exchanges, despite federal rules that initial purchase of qualified listed stocks may be effected for 65 per cent margin. Yet for years, shrewd speculators have been effecting highly leveraged positions at member firms using the good offices of those avid middlemen: the put-and-call dealers.

OTC Strategy

Interestingly, the same strategy may be effected when it comes to over-the-counter stocks which are *not* eligible for margin purposes under federal or Exchange margin regulations.

Several years back a former student of mine came to me with a problem. He had a position in 1,000 shares of a certain stock traded over-the-counter at the $50 level. He needed a good portion of his $50,000 to buy a certain desirable piece of income property. But having no desire to utterly lose his position in this alleged wonder stock, he wanted to buy the property and keep his stock at the same time. As a solution, he sold off his position and promptly replaced it by selling 10 puts on the OTC stock and buying 10 calls through an ac commodating put-and-call house. This released better than $30,000 in cash which he used to snare the coveted building. Since that time the stock has gone up to $115 bid—and the building has doubled in value. By doing this the operator was able to profit in both areas at the same time with his limited amount of money.

Some of the more discerning readers may immediately counter, "If this is so easy to do —and so simple—why doesn't everybody do it?"

Sadly so, the answer, "people do not know about this," doesn't fully apply here.

It applies only in part. There are stumbling blocks. The first stumbling block is the member firm of the New York Stock Exchange that carries the investor's margin account. This firm *must* be one that endorses put-and-call contracts. Not all Exchange members endorse puts and calls for their customers. So the investor's margin account must be at a member firm that endorses options. Second, although the *minimum* margin required under Exchange rules is a 25 per cent deposit, many firms that endorse options demand more than the minimum. These demands may range from 30 per cent (Green and Ladd) to 100 per cent (Kidder Peabody). In any event, before the investor attempts some trial conversions on his own he should ascertain both the margin requirements at the house that is handling his account and the basic fact that they are willing to guarantee, or endorse, the put contracts he intends to sell. The next—and most vital—thing the investor has to do is find a put-and-call dealer that will *accommodate him by using his put to create a call for him.* Because rates vary at various put-and-call firms it would be wise to determine beforehand what these self-aggrandizing people will charge for the service. From having done hundreds and hundreds of these conversions while working for Thomas Haab & Botts the charges generally seemed to emerge as about 2 per cent over the existing conversion money rate. In other words, if conversion money was 8 per cent per annum, the investor would pay about 10 per cent for the services. Currently, conversion money is about 7½ per cent; and so costs would probably run about 9 per cent per annum.

About Extensions

But the reader might ask what good is this if we are limited to six months? And the answer is the investor is not limited. Since he has issued the put and controls the call, he can *extend* the options on both sides of the transaction for another three months, six months, a year, etc., by paying an extension fee predicated upon the cost of conversion money.

"Aha," some reader might say. "If I own stock and it goes down I can stop out my mistake by dumping it. But what can I do if I have sold a put, own a call and the stock starts to go down. How can I protect myself?" And the answer is convert the call to a put to protect the outstanding put. Confusing? Probably, but since a put-and-call dealer can change a call to a put at will and a put to a call at will, he can also accommodate his customers by doing it for them at a fee or price. In this manner any investor who has sold a put and owns a call can protect himself.

Example 1: Put sold at $100; call owned at $100; market $90.

This leverage-minded operator doesn't care anymore about upside profits. He now wants to save what he has. He *converts* the call at $100 to a put at $100 through the good offices of a put-and-call dealer. Since the call at $100 is worthless when the stock is at $90, and since the put at $100 is worth $1,000 at $90, the investor must give the put-and-call dealer the call at $100 and $1,000 (plus a small charge). No matter how far down XYZ goes the investor is protected, because if the stock goes to $50 he is running the risk of being hit with 100 shares at $90 in his brokerage account by virtue of the outstanding put; but if he were to be hit with XYZ at $100 when the market is $50 he can exercise his own put at $100 —the put that was created for him when the dealer changed his worthless call into a protective put at the $100 level.

How much did the investor lose if the stock went to $50? He lost nothing more than he would have lost had he bought 100 shares of stock at $100, paid commissions, figured loss of interest on his $10,000 commitment and sold out at 90, paying commissions, etc.

And if after doing this, the stock had rallied and shot back to $120, the investor would have kicked himself mentally and physically, but he would have done the same had he owned Sinclair Oil at 65, sold it out at 75 after it had run up to 85 and dropped—and then helplessly watched it soar to $140.

But a pox on pessimism. After all most investors are incurable bulls. The bears have long since been impecuniated and forced to write books on how much they know about the market. So the bulls are in for profits, not losses. In this regard examine what happens to our conversion-minded friend if the stock goes up.

Example 2: Put sold at $100; call owned at $100; market $150.

The investor has done a six-month-ten-day conversion here and the market has soared within three months. He would be happy to cash in his call, but fears the market will react while he still has the outstanding put. What to do? Since the call at $100 is worth $5,000 at the 150 level and the put at $100 is worth nothing, the investor again can call upon that accommodating put-and-call dealer for action. This time the conversion game of put and take is played in reverse. The dealer gives the investor $5,000 (less a small charge) for the call and at the same time hands him a put at $100 which is worthless. *But this put will protect the put the investor has sold up to and including the last day of the contract.*

In effect, the investor has made precisely what he would have made had he bought 100 shares of XYZ at $100 through the good graces of a Swiss bank, carried it for the rise to $150 and liquidated.

Now there are many more maneuvers and many more pitfalls involved in the process of simulating ownership of a position via conversion. Space, of course, and perhaps the inability of the author to explain all the fine points, preclude further elaboration. But in summary, any red-blooded American over 21 can carry an owner's liability and reward in any stock in the land trading over $5 for as long as he likes with a deposit of only 25–30 per cent of the value per hundred share lot—without violating the rules of the Federal Reserve Board. As to specifically what the "small charges" are when put-and-call dealers accommodate their customers with protective or profit-taking maneuvers by changing puts into calls and calls into puts, it is enough to say that Larry Botts doesn't wear a $1,000–$20-gold-piece wrist watch because he won it at bingo or Monmouth Park. He made his bundle (bless him) from his business as all good American businessmen should. Trouble is who knows today what business any business is in? With conglomeration the new dictum and billions of dollars worth of paper blown out into the hands of the public by acquisition-minded, management-oriented, stock-market-profit-motivated management, who can tell for example what business Litton, Textron or Gulf & Western is in?

One thing is certain. While America was busy with Vietnam, with feeding Africa and India and with collecting the history of Lyndon B. Johnson at public expense, a group of brilliant traders made their pile merely by buying up American money!

···· **8** ····

The Hoarders

The almost universal—and not so funny —sentiment that there are more nuts walking around outside lunatic asylums than inside is dramatically illustrated by the bizarre happenings to everyday United States money—especially since President John F. Kennedy shivered through his coatless inauguration in January, 1961.

For it seems that right from the outset of the "new frontier" a myriad of amateur and professional hoarders went into action. Suddenly a paper dollar became worth more than a dollar. Nickels that contained a certain amount of a specific metal became worth 8¢ each. Coin shops erupted all over the face of the country "like measles in a girl's boarding school." Was it not completely crazy to walk down a New York City street in the year of our Lord 1968 and see for sale in one window after the other: a penny for 35¢, a nickel for 50¢, a dime for 75¢ and a dollar for $3?

Not only are these prices appended to small lots of even very recent pieces of specie and paper, but they are also tabbed on rolls of coins, bags of coins, bundles of bills, etc. In fact, the rash of coin dealers all over the land is linked up somewhat amorphously by a teletype system so that each major dealer can make a market on his own (and his competitor's) hoardings as they trade between each other and also with an avid, coin-collecting public.

So what has this to do with getting rich on other people's money? Plenty. Since the stock in trade of the hoarder is actually money, it makes perfectly fine collateral that can be used to borrow more ordinary money and buy more sought-after money that will increase in value.

Those Silver Certificates

By way of illustration, most people are aware that in June of the year LBJ decided to bow out of national politics those dollar bills bearing the legend promising to pay the bearer "one dollar in silver" had that promise *irrevocably* removed by a government that had long since begun to worry seriously about its stockpile of silver. But just before the 24th day of the month in which the government ended convertibility of silver certificates into the junior substitute for Midas metal the silver notes were commanding about $1.60 for each dollar's worth offered. Because of this, some smart people in Boston made a killing, using leverage. This perfectly legal scheme worked in this fashion.

A group of businessmen from the land of the bean and the cod got together and pooled a fund of $1 million. With this they quietly bought up silver certificates at a slight premium. Naturally, they could have held the bundle and waited for June, 1968, to arrive. But the profit would have been paltry after it was split several ways among the group. So they decided to *borrow* on the silver certificates. Naturally, *any* bank is willing to lend customers 100 per cent of the value of United States money deposited with them as collateral. The Bowery Savings Bank does it all the time, taking out full-page ads in metropolitan papers to bring to the attention of depositors that they can borrow from themselves at the Bowery far more reasonably interest-wise than they can from commercial banks or other loan sources. But it would have done these boys from Boston little good to take their $1 million in silver notes to a Boston or New York bank and borrow another million, because said banks as members of the Federal Reserve System were required to "turn in" all silver certificates appearing at the bank and substitute Federal Reserve notes (without any collateral at all behind them except the reputation of the country). So the Boston people went to the Swiss gnomes and hocked the silver certificates for a low-interest (6 per cent) loan. With this fresh million, the entrepreneurs bought up another bundle of silver certificates and repeated the process. So they had three million dollars in face value of silver certificates which remained safely in custody of the Swiss until it was time to resell them for a long-term capital gain. The group netted about 30¢ on the dollar after interest charges and thus cleared $900,000 in slightly more than six months merely by buying United States money. Since the Swiss were outside the pale of the federal regulations, they made apt custodians for the "good money" while readily lending the group ordinary money to buy more good bills.

While this was going on employees in banks were having a field day. All over the country the coin dealers—and even check-cashing services—were offering $1.25, $1.35, $1.45 for every dollar of face value on silver certificates in all denominations. The tellers would cull daily deposits for bills with blue ink on the seal, remove them from the bank during lunch, sell the bills to coin shops for premiums and replace the borrowed "lunch loan" with Federal Reserve notes that bore green seals. In this manner, enterprising bank employees were making as much as $500 a week from bank customers—but their superiors didn't seem to mind very much. Now that this bonanza has ended, bank employees have found another one in the five dollar bills that bear a red seal. These are currently worth about $8 when sold to coin shops.

Coins Mean Extra Cash

For many years employees at banks and other services that handle large amounts of specie (coins) have culled the influx for rare coins, and for coins that might have value both for collectors and for silver content.

Buffalo nickels are currently worth anywhere from 25¢ to $20 each if they are *uncirculated* —and circulated nickels are generally not wanted by the coin shops. But there was a time not so long ago when circulated Indian Head pennies brought no premium at all. Today they range from 8¢ each to more than $45 at the dealer—and collectors have to pay more in order to pay the dealer's overhead. Realizing this, many employees who handle money remove all coins that were minted under Presidencies that ascertained there was a suitable amount of silver and other precious metals in the innards of our coinage. Obviously, one rarely finds today a half-dollar or quarter or dime that is all in one piece and minted out of something of genuine value. Why? Because the government has retired all the silver coins that come into its agency banks and substituted ersatz (sand wich) coins. Yet with the mania of collectors, even some of this ersatz coinage will have extra value as the years pass—especially the uncirculated portion of the coinage.

So aspiring seekers of leverage have the choice of investing in the stock market, in the bond market, in paintings, antiques or stamps and coins. Since building a collection or operating a coin shop requires expertise and deep study, no one should undertake the task without two things:

1. Adequate preparation and study.
2. A source of continuing advice

Library shelves are crammed with books about coins and coin collecting. They also hold guides to current market value of currency and coins. Markets made by leading coin dealers are advertised in magazines devoted to numismatics and philately. And a study of the past indicates that fine coins rise in value as inflation hedges, in about the same proportion as the antique market grows via the vagaries of well-heeled collectors. It may be estimated that $50,000 invested in a good coin collection will double itself in five years. If the collection is in uncirculated United States money, it will always, of course, be worth at least face value. The chance of fine coins dropping in price as the population growth spawns millions of potential collectors is as slight as the author winning the Pulitzer prize for this book. So it may be safely held that investing in good coins after having received expert advice, or after having acquired a good self-education, is much *safer* than attempting to select stocks that will appreciate in the next five years.

Regrettably, the loans that are extended on collections of United States coins do not usually exceed the face value of the coins, so the leverage involved in using the good coins to borrow ordinary money to buy more good coins is limited—and the profits are eaten into by the interest charges on the loans. Understandably, loans cannot be acquired from Federal Reserve member banks because they would turn the good money right in to their district offices. Nor does it make any sense leveragewise to store the collection in a safe deposit box or with any other type of vault guardian. But money can

be borrowed on coin collections from the Provi-
dent Loan Society and other lenders such as
the Swiss and foreign bankers at rates running
as high as one per cent a month. If a collection
doubles in five years, it grows at the rate of 20
per cent a year. Obviously the leverage-minded
investor who can borrow at a cost of 12 per cent
per annum is coming out ahead by 8 per cent
on that part of his collection's value covered by
the loan.

When it comes to piling up a large collection
of uncirculated rolls and bags of silver dollars,
etc., the collection may become cumbersome and
involve storage costs.

Oh! Those Cartwheels

A handful of years back a New York broker
became enamored with Morgan dollars, commonly called cartwheels. He began to accumu-
late bags of these bulky circles of shimmering
silver for a premium of slightly more than the
value of the thousand silver dollars inside each
bag. In the process of buying up most of the
market in these dollars, he naturally forced the
price up—to $1,250, to $1,500 per bag, etc.
When the Johnson Administration began to feel
the onset of a silver "panic," the dollars became
avidly sought after because they contained
about $1.35 worth of silver at going government
market prices. Lo and behold, the broker con-
jured up a brainstorm and began to use his
stockpile as a basis for buying and selling bags
of Morgan dollars on the New York Mercantile
Exchange as an integrated part of that arena's

commodity futures trading program. And the dollars shot up to $2,000, to $2,250 and higher per bag.

Dismayed by the continuing shortage of silver in his government's stockpile, an official recently proposed that Uncle Sam—in the guise of Richard Nixon—sell off the 3,000,000 Morgan dollars held in storage and owned by the government. If the government were to auction off its hoardings in cartwheels, claims this official, it will net better than $29,000,000, or better than $9 a cartwheel!

Profits from Hoarding

Obviously there are deterrents to this sensible plan to have the government make a windfall profit on its own money: (1) How would it show the gain on its books? and (2) How would this help its worsening silver shortage?

The moral of all this, of course, is that when one possesses something of value which other people want, the price goes up. In the coin market as elsewhere, the price is usually made by the person most anxious to do the business.

Profits from hoarding exist with other interesting items such as stamps, antiques, art and even wine.

Stamps have enough books written about them that they do not have to be belabored here. It might be mentioned in passing that any time anyone ever decides to leave a country and is not permitted to take cash or worldly goods of value, the best thing to do is to turn the available cash into fine stamps and ship them off to relatives in the country of expected residence. This was one of the methods resorted to by harassed Jews who wanted to escape from Nazi Germany with more than their own skins.

About Antiques

Antiques are a multi-faceted collector's nightmare and should not be entered into readily by people who might be broadly classed "dilettantes." The same goes for art. And it might be noted that in the past well-heeled collectors of works of art fared better from the tax break than they did from the puffed up prices created in the art market by their own activities. For example, Billy Rose when he reached 60 began to worry about dying. To insure himself a modicum of pleasure in his afterlife he donated about $5,000,000 worth of art to Israel. This princely sum represented a tax deduction. As a result, since he was obviously in the top bracket, Uncle Sam shared 70 cents on the dollar with the gift. The $3,500,000 tax break exceeded by far the actual cost of the works of art involved when acquired. But they were *worth* $5,000,000 at the time of the gift. That is why, perhaps, our museums all over the country have flourished through donations of art works, which if not kept in the museum collections are sold to private collectors who eventually will give them to other museums as tax deductions.

For leverage seekers, however, antiques and works of art do not hold forth as much promise as do other areas of possible appreciation. The main reason is that sources of available loan money on antiques and art are of necessity *extremely* limited—and, in fact, may be almost exclusively relegated to private lenders or hock shops. But one area of growing interest abetted by the inherent lunacy that currently besets collection-crazy America is wine.

Vineyard Profits

When Governor Tilden gave up the ghost in 1886, his executors promptly sold off his wine cellar. The backbone of Governor Tilden's collection consisted of "10 cases Steinberger Cabinet (1862) and 19 cases Johannesberger Blue Seal (1862)." At the time the going price for these rare vintages was $45 a case for the Steinberger and $85 a case for the Johannesberger. Undoubtedly, a case of each of these wines today would bring a king's ransom. And the lucky millionaire, who prides himself on his acquired ability as a sommelier, may boast of a wine cellar which has tripled or quadrupled in value in the last twenty years. But sparked by interest fostered in the ivy-covered walls of academe, good wine (French or German, of course, how can anything else be called wine?) is being rapidly acquired for investment purposes by the same kinds of discerning profit-seekers who jumped into the coin market at its early—and not so crazy—stages.

A case of wine from Governor Tilden's time that today commands a handsome increase in price is quite understandable—and even forgivable. But what about wines bottled in 1959, in 1961, in 1966?

If bought in 1962, a case of Chateau Petrus sold for $75 to the wine-sipping public. In 1968, the tab per case for the same wine was $235, or better than triple its original retail price. Haut Brion, bottled in 1966, was sold the following year to aficionados of Bacchus' bliss for $79.50. A year later it reached $100 a case. In a few years, insists one of New York City's leading wine merchants, the wine will retail for more than $200 a case. In 1960, a bottle of rather ordinary wine of 1959 vintage sold for $2.50. Today the same bottle sells for $30, or 12 times as much. Experts claim an investment in "almost any name wine from France or Germany appreciates automatically every year." And if it doesn't? The hoarder can always drink it, or give it away for Christmas.

Investing in wines for future profitable resale, however, is a ticklish business. Wines cannot be resold to the public except through licensed liquor dealers. In this regard the investor comes up against the same thing he encounters in the coin market and the over-the-counter stock market, he has to deal with intermediaries and is often at their mercy if they are forced to inventory the items to be sold.

A second deterrent to most serious-minded investors who seek such a sure thing is the fact that wines if not stored properly will spoil. In New York City there are some 20 warehouses willing to store wines for customers—with a standard rate of 20 cents per case per month. But most of all, the objection for the leverage-seeker is that he cannot borrow enough on his wine purchases to buy more wine. One would think in the face of such a sure thing as an annual appreciation of selected vintages and brands that banks would be cooperative. But they are not. And many erstwhile investors, once bitten by the wine-collecting bug eventually forget their original germane intentions and become "connoisseurs." To their friends, these dedicated people will say, "The best thing about investing in wines is that they appreciate over the years. But I'm not selling."

But the real leverage for people interested in wines is not centered upon the collection of bottles filled with bubbly or Chablis. The secret of real leverage lies in the vineyard.

Many of the moneyed people in the United States already own vineyards. This aspect involves buying the vineyard and hocking it. Then assuming that the vineyard produces a maximum of 15,000 cases a year, the vineyard will sell off 10,000 cases and hold back 5,000 from the market. By doing this over a period of years, the vineyard can command enormous profits on its production as the values of its wines increase. Meanwhile, the *whole* thing is operated and financed by bank money. *Warning:* Do not buy American vineyards—only German or French. In America the grape pickers can make serious trouble for the vineyard owners. And for the average man of means who does not have the proper connections to buy foreign real estate, perhaps the sentiments of the president of Chanel are appropriate: "A bottle of wine has no value until it is opened and drunk."

The Art Mania

In summary, the main problem that besets any hoarder is the realization that at any time he sells off fine art, good coins, sought-after stamps, select vintages, etc. the replacement prices zoom for comparable merchandise. Moreover, had the entrepreneur held on for another year, another six months, etc., he would have received assuredly a higher price as the pressure from increasing numbers of American collectors keeps pushing prices higher and higher. And just as in the market, price-earnings yardsticks are lengthened almost every year; the yardsticks judging innate value of objects of art, etc., alter. Maybe the enterprising man earlier in this book who ran back and forth between the bank, the broker and the real estate office should stop on the way at an art gallery, an antique shop, a liquor store and stock up on valuable items as cushions against down markets. Who knows? But it is good to follow Bernard Baruch's advice. He said, "I never cross my bridges till I get to them, but I like to lay down a few pontoons first." His "pontoons" included measures of protection.

Every sensible investor should consider methods of protection to his committed capital—especially those daring souls who try to get rich on borrowed money.

····· 9 ·····

Profits—With Protection

A retailer buys $10,000 worth of sneakers and expects to make at least 20 per cent on the lot after taxes. But what if the public does not buy, and he does not sell off the entire shipment? Obviously, not only does he stand the chance of failing to realize his predetermined profit goal, but he may also wind up with a loss if he is forced to liquidate his inventory to raise cash to invest in something profitable. Can he limit his loss? Insure himself that come what may his $10,000 will only deteriorate to $9,000, or $8,500? Of course not. No one enterprising enough has as yet figured out price insurance. And the retailer must take his risks—without being able to protect his principal from severe price deterioration.

Price Protection

Oddly enough, the stock market is one of the few arenas in the world of trade where sensible speculators — especially leveraged ones — can limit their losses to a predetermined percentage of their monetary commitment. Remember the enterprising young man who inveigled his mother-in-law into lending him $6,500 so he could carry 200 shares of Big Telephone on 35 per cent margin at an accommodating bank? If he had bought Telephone at $50, the bank would have been protected for only 17½ points on the downside. Undoubtedly, if Telephone sank to $45, the bank would have been calling the leveraged chap for perhaps $500 of margin maintenance money. But there is a way in which the young man with million-dollar ideas could protect his leveraged purchase so that no matter which way Telephone went he would limit his loss to a preset figure. *At the time he buys his 200 shares of Telephone he simultaneously buys two puts for ninety days.*

In this manner, if Telephone rises, the puts will be considered as insurance and will be, of course, worthless. But if Telephone drops, the owner of the puts can deliver the shares he purchased at the $50 level (less, of course, his cost of buying the puts).

Assume the investor paid $250 for each ninety-day put. His total cost of protecting his highly levered position for the three-month period would be $500. If a prolonged market decline set in during that time and Telephone dropped to the incredible price of $35 a share, the protected investor would have lost $500 instead of $3,000.

Because of a beneficent government, speculators and investors in the stock market who seek long-term capital gains are permitted to establish a protected position; hold for the six-month + required period and sell at a profit which is long-term gain, even though the investor was completely protected during that period against downside loss.

For example, an investor positions 100 shares of XYZ trading at $100 a share and simultaneously buys a six-month-ten-day put on XYZ at $100 for a money cost (premium) of $900. By the end of the period of the put the market price of XYZ is $200. The investor who has hedged his position with the put sells out at $200 and considers his cost for tax purposes as $109 a share ($100, purchase price, plus $9 a share cost of the put). But if XYZ instead of climbing had plummeted to $50, the investor could have put the shares (delivered them) at the $100 level, less the $9 per share cost of the put, or $91. In other words, for $900 the leverage-minded or cash-minded investor seeking *protected* long-term capital gains on $10,000, can insure his holdings for the required period, if he buys puts to protect his position on the same day that he assumes said position—and holds the position for the statutory seasoning period.

Stock Market Insurance

Another method of protecting listed positions is the stop-loss order, which at best puts the investor in the position of playing the market against professionals (specialists) armed with "marked cards." Suppose the sensible investor who seeks to safeguard principal while attempting to attain profits was reluctant to shell out the $900 for a protective put at the time he purchased 100 XYZ at $100. He could have entered a stop-loss order to sell the shares at 91. If the stock had moved up instead of down the investor could have moved up his stop—keeping it nine or ten points behind the market, at no out-of-pocket costs.

But this theory is perfectly wonderful when the stock is listed and in markets where it takes more than a single trading session for an issue to fluctuate ten per cent. There were times when quality stocks didn't fluctuate between their highs and lows in an entire year as much as ten per cent. But in the fast-moving markets which have featured speculation on the New York and American Stock Exchanges during the past handful of years, entering stop orders nine or ten per cent under the market may find the position "touched off," sold out—and suddenly a rally comes in during the very same trading session sending the stock higher than it was before it began to drop to set off the stop. Because a stop-loss order becomes a market order when the price of the stock reaches—or goes through—the stop, the investor is never sure he will get precisely what he anticipates when he enters the stop order. Thus, if our conservative speculator protected his position of 100 XYZ at $100 with a stop-loss sell order at 91 and the market began to fall, he could wind up getting 89 or 88 if the price plummeted through his 91 stop—without trading at 91.

In the case of the investor who paid out $900 for a put at $100, he is absolutely guaranteed the 91 level no matter how far down the price of the stock in question might drop during the life of his put option.

The only disenchantment with the use of puts for protection is that unlike the stop order the effective price of the put does not change, while an investor, of course, can raise his stop limit if the price of the subject shares soars.

At this point anyone who has had the least bit of experience with puts and calls will ask himself, "If I buy 100 shares of XYZ at $100, leverage it for 70 per cent in the form of a special-purpose loan and then have to pay for a protective put, where am I?" It pays to examine this situation:

Cost of carrying loan for six months=	$350.00
Cost of protective put =	900.00
Out-of-pocket costs	$1,250
Margin money needed	3,000
Total out-of-pocket cash for a fully pro-tected—and highly levered—position $4,250	

But the stock has to move up at least 12½ points during the six-month period merely for the investor to recoup his costs, before in-and-out commissions and taxes of roughly $100.

And if the stock does move up 12½ points, the investor is then gaining at the rate of $100 a point on an out-of-pocket cash outlay of $4,250. In other words, instead of being margined at 30 per cent, he is margined at 42 per cent—with a *total possible loss* of $1,250, or 12½ per cent of the total of $10,000 risked.

There must be a better way—*and there is. Never* buy stock—hock it—and protect it. It makes much more sense to simply buy a call.

Protected Leverage

Assume that the same investor had read this book and liked XYZ at $100. Instead of worrying about artful dodges like the bank-and-mother-in-law-and-broker bit, and instead of bothering about stop-loss orders or protective puts, he never bought the stock at all; but he was still anxious to profit from high leverage on XYZ's anticipated rise. And assuming that sensibly so he also wanted to limit his risk to 12½ per cent or less no matter how far down the shares of XYZ might go if he were to dabble in an attempt to make a long-term capital gain through the price movement of XYZ shares, he would *never* buy 100 XYZ. Instead he would buy a six-month-10-day call on 100 XYZ at $100 for a money cost (premium) of $1,150 (plus $5 tax). In so doing, the investor acquires an *option* to buy 100 XYZ at $100 at *any time* during the next six months and 10 days no matter where the actual market in XYZ shares might be. Thus if XYZ shot up to $200 and the investor had the right to buy 100 shares of XYZ at 100, how much would that right be worth? At least $10,000. At this point the investor has the option to either position his shares at the $10,000 cost when they are worth $20,000, or he can *resell* his option for its value.

Consider the position of the intelligent investor who controls the price action of 100 shares of XYZ for six months via a call.

His out-of-pocket outlay is $1,150—a hundred dollars in costs less than the fellow who leverages a long position in a special-purpose loan and protects it with a put. Moreover, his total risk is $1,150. If the stock shoots up to $200 he has potentially a gross profit of $8,950, less in-and-out commissions (to buy 100 shares at 100 when call is exercised and to sell 100 XYZ at $200 simultaneously, including the $5 Rockefeller-Lindsay tax). Now what if the stock declines to $50 and stays there for six months? Simple. The call becomes worthless (dies or expires), the investor gets a tax loss of $1,150 which can be applied against realized capital gains, or against $1,000 a year in income in the absence of established off-setting capital gains.

The sensibility of this type of stock market risk-taking began during the courses the author inaugurated at the Biltmore Hotel in November, 1957, and ran continuously for the next decade.* Thousands upon thousands of leverage-minded —and intelligent investors—flocked to buy calls instead of stock because calls make so much more sense.

The advantages to people who are interested in investing instead of speculating are also almost immediately obvious. If a person really wants to buy 100 XYZ at $100 and buys a six-month call instead, he can sit back and watch the issue during that time. *He controls it just as if he actually owns the 100-share lot.* Assume that at the end of the six-month period XYZ

---

* For information about the author's next course, write directly to him.

is $150, the sensible investor can now call the shares at $100 (exercise his call) and place them in his account at a cost of $100 plus the $11.50 per-share-call-cost, or a basis cost of 111½ for tax purposes. *But if XYZ declined to $50* during the term of the call, all the investor would have lost is the cost of the call—and not the $5,000 on paper he would be locked in with if he had bought the shares the regular way.

Downside Insurance

Meanwhile, one way to keep from being wiped out in an overbought market is to *protect everything* with downside insurance. Either use puts to protect existing long positions, or use calls to assume simulated new positions. In either event, the loss is limited—fixed in advance—and the door to further profits left wide open.

Remember: purchase of a long position in the stock market initiates risk. It makes sense to limit the risk at all times—especially if the risk has been assumed to a large degree with other people's money. And now for a peek at the opportunities in the money market.

···· 10 ····

Leveraging the
Money Market

At this writing the government owes
investment bankers, institutions, and
individual creditors in excess of $350
billion. And the annual interest payments
on its debt are approaching $20 billion.
The interest payments alone represent
annual expenditures in excess of *all* the
government debt in history from the
time of the first Continental Congress to
the entrance of HST into the White
House when FDR passed out of our
national scene so abruptly. Our government, in acquiring such an astounding
burden of debt combined with annual
interest, has created an ever increasing
floating debt. The floating debt is merely
the volume of government securities that
mature within the space of a single year.

To meet this debt the government issues other securities, "rolling over" the debt that comes due into more debt.

The securities the government issues to meet its floating debt obligations vary in nature and in maturity dates. They can either be bonds (sold with semi-annual interest payments), Treasury Bills (sold at a discount from face value), notes (obligations that are interest-bearing) or agency obligations (bonds or notes of agencies of the federal government).

And during the administration of the tall man from Texas his money market people invented participations, in which certificates representing existing agency debt were laid off to investors to permit the refinancing of existing government debt while said debt was still in existence—or to put it bluntly, a sort of a second borrowing on the same collateral.

Debt Instrument Mix

But why all the complexity of the various kinds of debt instruments? The answer, incredibly so, is that this creates opportunities for alert speculators and risk-takers to profit from leveraged operations in government debt securities.

There exists an archaic regulation or law which prohibits Uncle Sam from paying more than $4\frac{1}{4}$ per cent interest per annum on bonds it decides to float. But it has been almost ages since the debt market rates for bonds of this nature could have been sold at face value for such a low rate. Money commanded 5 per cent, then 6 per cent, then 8, etc., as the price for it rose along with increasing demand from all sources. And so as long-term bonds came due, the government was compelled to "roll them over" into shorter term securities that were not bonds, but rather debt instruments which were more competitive interest-rate-wise with existing market conditions. Most of the government refunding efforts in this regard centered upon Treasury Bills.

Those Treasury Bills

Treasury Bills are short-term obligations of the federal government that bear varying maturities up to one year and are sold at a discount. For example, at the weekly auction of the Federal Reserve Board in the New York District a lot of one-year Bills may be sold at 95. This means dealers who specialize in such debt instruments will pay $950 per $1,000 face value of the Bills. If held to the last day, the owner of the Bill at 95 will receive its face value of 100, or the $950 invested with Uncle Sam would earn $50. This is, of course, a higher return than had the investor bought an obligation of the government with face value of $1,000, held it for one year, and received his $1,000 back plus interest of $50. In this case his interest rate would be 5 per cent per annum. But the investor who buys a Bill at 95 and holds for a year earns 5.6 per cent if he redeems the Bill at maturity for $1,000.

Now each Treasury Bill becomes more valuable with each passing day as it heads toward maturity. And the mathematically inclined investor can readily calculate the yield and the rate of increase per day, presuming that interest rates remained stable from the time he bought the bill until maturity. *But interest rates do not remain stable.* In the case of Treasury Bills, the growth rate of equity for the investor waiting for maturity will decelerate if interest rates rise and accelerate if interest rates decline. Because of this—and because of a combination of very high leverage coupled with low commissions—some speculators have made killings in Treasury Bills by buying them at the right time, hocking them during periods of low interest rates, and selling them when money gets tight.

Students of the money market know that there are, or at least have been for ages, periods of rise and fall in interest rates. Catching the swing by buying existing Bills in a high interest rate market and (after hocking them for *five cents on the dollar*) reselling them when interest rates fall is one of the most cherished dreams of money men. Another interesting maneuver is to buy existing United States bonds of the negotiable type that are trading well below par because of low interest coupon rate during high interest rate markets and selling the bonds as the principal rises when interest rates fall. Here again the bonds may be hocked for as little as five to ten cents on the dollar.

A Case in Governments

Assume that a leverage-minded student of money markets decides that at this writing the current interest rates are about as high as they are likely to get during the next six months. With the prime money rate at 6½ per cent, a person seeking leverage from banks or brokers on government obligations would have to pay between 7¼ and 7½ per cent per annum. Because of the expense of carrying a leveraged position that obviously will not earn enough to pay interest charges, most leverage seekers would shy away. But this daring lad decides he is in it for *gain* rather than return; and so he buys $1,000,000 worth of 3¼, 1978, United States bonds currently yielding 5.51 per cent because of their price of about 77. To swing his million in bonds the enterprising investor needs about $37,500. Voilà! He is now in a position where his annual interest payments will exceed his annual interest intake by about 2 per cent, or a potential loss of about $14,650 a year.

For most investors who habitually trade in government bonds this loss is income deductible. But it must be clearly understood that those enterprising souls who seek to dabble in government bonds to set up losses in order to mitigate their tax bills may find the deductions disallowed all the way up to the Tax Court.

Now if the investor were solely interested in leveraging his bonds for tax purposes he would (in the example mentioned) readily pony up the loss each year to the bank or broker in question; and at the time the 3¼'s of 1978 approach maturity and are trading at par, he can resell them for a long-term capital gain. This is how his situation would look if such a maneuver were followed:

Purchase in 1968	$770,000
10-year loss @ $14,650 a year	146,500

Sale at par, 1978	$1,000,000
Gross profit	230,000
Less commissions	2,500
	$227,500
Less loss on interest	146,500
Before Tax Profit=	$81,000

Interestingly, this profit of $81,000 is long term and can net the investor a *minimum* of $60,750 during the ten-year period on his risk of $37,500 (plus the annual interest deficit). But it's a *sure thing*. The investor cannot lose if he holds to maturity. He can only lose if interest rates rise radically after he has made his purchase and he decides to sell out at a loss, or if Uncle Sam decides the losses the speculator took were not deductible because of an ill-veiled subterfuge to "cheat" the government out of taxes due.

Now assume that the investor was not looking for a combination of ten years of tax loss and one year of capital long-term gain. But that he instead sought profits in the same year he makes his commitment. He buys, in December, 1968, a million in face of the same maturity, plunking down $37,500. He also has set himself up to lose $14,650 a year because of the differential in the amount of interest he receives as a bondholder and what he is forced to pay by virtue of having borrowed 95 per cent to carry his position. But several months after the investor has saddled himself so uncomfortably, the new President's Treasury secretary performs the expected miracle and forces interest rates down. Immediately the *value* of the 3¼'s rise to match the variations in going interest rates.

Our speculator sees his holdings move up to 87 —and he sells. How does he come out in the three-month period?

Loss for three months' interest differential	=	$3,562
Commissions	=	2,500
Total expenses	=	$6,062
Profit on position before expenses	=	$100,000
Less expenses	=	6,062
Profit before taxes	=	$93,938

Now it is not to be construed that bond rates will necessarily cause such a wide fluctuation in prices of existing obligations, but suppose the decline in the prime rate had gone from 6½ per cent to 4 per cent, and the investor's bonds had moved up from 77 to 82, instead of 87. He still would have made better than $45,000 in three months, or better than 100 per cent on his deposit in the *safest* securities in the world: obligations of the United States of America.

On pages 140 and 141 is a listing of government and agency obligations for Friday, December 13, 1968. Check the prices they are at today. See for yourself what 20/20 hindsight can do.

Of course, it could possibly be that interest rates will continue to get even higher—despite Mr. Nixon's excellent choice for the Treasury secretaryship. And if this were the case, the enterprising speculator who leaped into the 3¼'s of 1978 on a shoestring might find himself being called for more margin, or wiped out.

Currency Hedging

George Bockl who penned one of the most entertaining and edifying books on leveraging

U.S. Treas. Bills

Mat	Bid Discount	Ask Discount	Mat	Bid Discount	Ask Discount
12-19	5.85	4.91	4-10	5.91	5.76
12-26	5.60	4.90	4-17	5.91	5.77
12-31	5.50	4.85	4-22	5.92	5.87
1- 2	5.55	5.10	4-24	5.92	5.79
1- 9	5.55	5.15	4-30	5.91	5.76
1-16	5.62	5.28	5- 1	5.93	5.78
1-23	5.70	5.40	5- 8	5.93	5.79
1-30	5.72	5.48	5-15	5.93	5.79
1-31	5.70	5.45	5-22	5.94	5.80
2- 6	5.83	5.63	5-29	5.94	5.80
2-13	5.89	5.71	5-31	5.93	5.79
2-20	5.90	5.72	6- 5	5.93	5.85
2-27	5.90	5.73	6-12	5.94	5.90
2-28	5.87	5.65	6-23	5.94	5.91
3- 6	5.87	5.78	6-30	5.96	5.84
3-13	5.88	5.84	7-31	5.92	5.78
3-20	5.89	5.77	8-31	5.90	5.86
3-24	5.85	5.77	9-30	5.93	5.76
3-27	5.89	5.74	10-31	5.92	5.76
3-31	5.88	5.73	11-30	5.81	5.77
4- 3	5.91	5.76			

Treasury Bonds

				Bid	Asked	Bid Chg.	Yld.
4s,	1969	Feb.	....	99.20	99.22	...	5.86
2½s,	1964-69	June	....	98.19	98.23	− .1	5.16
4s,	1969	Oct.	....	98.20	98.24	+ .1	5.62
2½s,	1964-69	Dec.	....	97.13	97.17	a	5.06
2½s,	1965-70	Mar.	....	96.20	96.24	+ .1	5.23
4s,	1970	Feb.	....	98.1	98.5	+ .2	5.66
4s,	1970	Aug.	....	97.6	97.10	+ .2	5.72
2½s,	1966-71	Mar.	....	94.6	94.14	...	5.16
4s,	1971	Aug.	....	95.19	95.27	+ .1	5.70
3⅞s,	1971	Nov.	....	94.29	95.5	+ .1	5.70
4s,	1972	Feb.	....	94.21	94.29	+ .3	5.78
2½s,	1967-72	June	....	90.30	91.6	+ .2	5.29
4s,	1972	Aug.	....	93.31	94.7	+ .1	5.77
2½s,	1967-72	Sept.	....	90.11	90.19	+ .2	5.30
2½s,	1967-72	Dec.	....	89.28	90.4	+ .2	5.27
4s,	1973	Aug.	....	92.24	93.0	+ .2	5.74
4⅛s,	1973	Nov.	....	92.28	93.4	+ .2	5.76
4⅛s,	1974	Feb.	....	92.23	92.31	+ .2	5.71
4¼s,	1974	May	....	92.29	93.5	+ .3	5.74
3⅞s,	1974	Nov.	....	91.10	91.18	+ .2	5.57
4s,	1980	Feb.	....	84.22	85.6	...	5.82
3½s,	1980	Nov.	....	80.28	81.12	...	5.67
3¼s,	1978-83	June	....	77.4	77.20	...	5.51
3¼s,	1985	May	....	75.24	76.8	...	5.46
4¼s,	1975-85	May	....	83.20	84.4	...	5.75
3½s,	1990	Feb.	....	74.8	74.24	+ .2	5.54
4¼s,	1987-92	Aug.	....	79.8	79.24		5.84
4s,	1988-93	Feb.	....	77.24	78.8	− .4	5.66
4⅛s,	1989-94	May	....	77.24	78.8	− .2	5.77
3s,	1995	Feb.	....	73.30	74.14	+ .2	4.71
3½s,	1998	Nov.	....	77.4	77.20	+ .2	5.17

U.S. Treas. Notes

Rate	Mat	Bid	Asked	Yld
5⅝	2-69	99.29	99.31	5.71
1½	4-69	98.20	98.28	5.45
5⅝	5-69	99.26	99.28	5.91
6	8-69	99.31	100.3	5.86
1½	10-69	97.8	97.16	4.76
1½	4-70	95.20	96.0	4.73
5⅝	5-70	99.18	99.20	5.91
1½	10-70	94.4	94.8	4.89
5	11-70	98.5	98.9	5.97
5⅜	2-71	98.22	98.30	5.91
1½	4-71	92.16	92.30	4.79
5¼	5-71	98.9	98.17	5.91
1½	10-71	90.26	91.26	4.66
5⅜	11-71	98.18	98.26	5.82
4¾	2-72	96.6	96.14	6.00
1½	4-72	89.10	90.10	4.71
4¾	5-72	96.0	96.8	5.98
1½	10-72	87.26	88.26	4.76
1½	4-73	86.10	87.10	4.81
1½	10-73	85.0	86.0	4.81
5⅝	8-74	97.22	97.26	6.09
5¾	11-74	98.13	98.17	6.05
5¾	2-75	98.15	98.23	6.01
6	5-75	100.1	100.9	5.95

Federal Land Bank

Rate	Mat	Bid	Asked	Yld
4⅛	2-72-67	93.24	94.24	5.97
4½	10-70-67	96.24	97.24	5.84
5.95	12-68	99.31	100.0	5.78
4¾	1-69	99.22	99.30	5.33
4⅜	3-69	99.4	99.20	5.79
5.60	4-69	99.24	99.28	5.92
4¼	7-69	98.4	99.4	5.81
4⅝	7-69	98.8	99.8	5.96
6¼	9-69	99.28	100.4	6.06
4¼	10-69	98.0	99.0	5.47
5¾	1-70	99.12	99.28	5.86
5⅛	2-70	98.0	99.0	6.01
6.30	2-70	100.0	100.16	5.84
3½	4-70	96.16	97.16	5.53
6.20	4-70	99.24	100.8	6.00
5⅛	7-70	97.24	98.24	5.96
6.00	7-70	99.16	99.28	6.08
6.30	10-70	100.0	100.4	6.22
3½	5-71	94.8	95.8	5.67
6.00	10-71	99.10	99.18	6.17
5.70	2-72	98.4	98.20	6.18
3⅞	9-72	92.8	93.8	5.91
5⅞	10-72	98.24	99.24	5.95
4⅛	2-78-73	85.24	86.24	6.03
4½	2-74	92.0	93.0	6.10
4⅜	4-75	90.8	91.8	6.06
5	2-76	93.8	94.8	6.00
5⅜	7-76	95.24	96.24	5.91
5⅛	4-78	91.16	92.16	6.18
5	1-79	90.4	91.4	6.19

World Bank Bonds

Rate	Mat	Bid	Asked	Yld
3½	1969	99.0	99.24	6.05
5⅜	1969	99.0	100.0	5.38
5¾	1969	98.24	99.24	6.10
6⅛	1970	99.0	100.0	6.13
5.80	1970	98.16	99.16	6.20
3½	1971	91.24	92.24	6.35
3	1972	90.16	91.16	5.66
4½	1973	91.0	93.0	6.15
3⅜	1975	84.0	85.16	6.15
3	1976	82.0	84.0	5.67
4½	1977	84.16	86.16	6.69
4¼	1978	81.0	83.0	6.70
4¼	1979	81.0	83.0	6.59
4¾	1980	84.0	86.0	6.45
3¼	1981	75.0	77.0	5.82
4½	1982	79.16	81.16	6.63
5	1985	82.0	84.0	6.63
4½	1990	74.0	76.0	6.60
5⅜	1991	81.16	83.16	6.82
5⅜	1992	81.16	83.16	6.80
5⅞	1993	86.16	88.16	6.85
6½	1994	93.16	95.16	6.88
6⅝	1994	92.0	94.0	6.88

Fd'l Home Loan Bk.

Rate	Mat	Bid	Asked	Yld
5½	1-69	99.29	99.31	5.66
5.85	2-69	99.28	99.30	5.96
5.65	2-69	99.27	99.29	6.05
5⅜	3-69	99.20	99.28	5.77
6.25	4-69	99.30	100.0	6.04
6.00	5-69	99.26	99.28	6.15
6.30	6-69	100.0	100.2	6.17
5¾	7-69	99.21	99.23	6.15
6.00	9-69	99.20	99.28	6.15
6.00	11-69	99.25	99.27	6.17
6.00	2-70	99.22	99.30	6.04
6.00	3-70	99.22	99.30	6.04
6.00	4-70	99.22	99.30	6.04
5.80	5-70	99.15	99.19	6.09

FIC Bank Debs.

Rate	Mat	Bid	Asked	Yld
5.95	1- 2	99.31	100.1	4.99
6.10	2- 3	99.30	100.0	5.88
6.45	3- 3	100.0	100.2	5.94
6.25	4- 1	99.29	99.31	6.18
5.95	5- 1	99.26	99.28	6.16
5.65	6- 2	99.21	99.23	6.18
5⅝	7- 1	99.20	99.22	6.15
5.80	8- 4	99.22	99.24	6.17
6.05	9- 2	99.27	99.29	6.17

Inter-Amer. Devel. Bk.

Rate	Mat	Bid	Asked	Yld
4¼	12-82	78.0	80.0	6.44
4½	4-84	79.0	81.0	6.4
4½	11-84	79.0	81.0	6.43
5.20	1-92	82.0	84.0	6.56
6½	11-92	96.0	97.0	6.76
6⅝	11-93	97.0	98.0	6.79

FNMA Notes & Debs.

Rate	Mat	Bid	Asked	Yld
4⅜	4-69	99.10	99.18	5.75
4.65	5-69	99.11	99.15	5.97
6.10	6-69	99.29	100.1	6.03
5⅛	7-69	99.12	99.16	6.03
6	12-69	99.20	100.0	6.00
4⅝	4-70	97.24	98.8	6.02
6.60	6-70	100.4	100.20	6.15
4⅛	9-70	96.20	97.4	5.89
5¾	10-70	99.0	99.16	6.04
6	3-71	99.0	99.16	6.24
4⅛	8-71	94.24	95.20	5.93
5¾	9-71	98.4	98.20	6.30
4½	9-71	95.4	96.4	6.06
5⅛	2-72	96.12	97.12	6.05
4⅜	6-72	93.16	94.16	6.15
4¼	6-73	91.16	92.16	6.19
4½	2-77	88.16	89.16	6.16

Bank for Co-ops

Rate	Mat	Bid	Asked	Yld
6.20	1-69	99.31	100.1	5.30
6.00	2-69	99.30	100.0	5.87
5.55	4-69	99.24	99.26	6.14
5.80	5-69	99.25	99.27	6.19
6.05	6-69	99.29	99.31	6.10

with real estate warns "Living with leverage is like living on a knife's edge." It takes intestinal fortitude to assume risks with leverage, even if the investments are securities of the United States of America. In this regard, there has recently developed a breed of speculators who are convinced that the United States dollar will be *devalued*. To secure profits they have sold the dollar short against Swiss francs or German marks. How can one do this?

It all comes from hedging. Assume a steel supplier in the United States sold $500,000 worth of I-beams to a Portuguese construction company—and was to be paid in escudos at the time of delivery (three months from date of the order). To protect himself from possible devaluation of the escudo in the interim, the distributor sells $500,000 worth of escudos at current convertibility into dollars "short" (forward sale for three months). In this manner he has assured himself of not being open to any monetary loss due to fluctuations in foreign exchange, because he has sold one currency against another: a strong currency against an allegedly weak one. If the weak currency collapses through devaluation, the distributor will profit from his short sale sufficiently to cover inroads against his invoice. If the strong currency gets stronger, it makes little difference to the distributor because all he is interested in is getting $500,000 worth of *value* at the time his goods go overseas.

This, of course, is an example of legitimate forward sale of monies to protect adverse changes in foreign exchange. But there is a veritable horde of speculators at home and abroad who have been making forward sales of one currency against the other in order to profit from price fluctuations. Every time the English pound was devalued somebody alert made a cleanup. If the French franc had been devalued in December of 1968 other killings in foreign exchange would have been effected. And when it eventually is devalued, those intransigent but brave souls who rush in to clobber a country's currency will find a windfall.

Inflation Dollars

Naturally, in all of this most people assume the dollar is sacrosanct. Well it is, in every place except purchasing power. The story goes that a latter-day investor fell asleep after he had positioned 100 T, 100 GE and 100 XRX. Like Rip Van Winkle, he thereafter slept for 100 years. Upon his return to the world of the living, the "young" man promptly called his broker to find out how his holdings stood. "How's my Telephone?" he asked. And the answer came, "It's worth $8,500,000." "And My GE?" "It's worth $12,500,000." "And Xerox?" "Say! That's worth $35,000,000."

"My God," shouted the happy investor, "I'm rich. I'm rich."

Just then the operator interrupted with: "I'm sorry sir. Your three minutes are up. Deposit $10,000,000 for the next five minutes. . . ."

Indeed we live in a world of dollar erosion where the poor, the middle-class and even the rich find themselves clobbered between rising prices and rising taxes. No longer is our land as Lincoln said a country by, of and for the people. It is a land for the corporations only.

So maybe before trying to do anything at all about leverage trading, form a corporation. And this is why.

Maximum tax on corporations today is 48 per cent: personal top is 60 per cent. Corporations can deduct all losses from income the same year. Taxpayers can only take off $1,000 in losses each year in the absence of profits. Certain securities are 85 per cent exempt income-wise from taxes for corporations. Individuals have to pay on all income over the dividend pittance they are now allotted.

Most of all corporations benefit from depreciation. It is recorded that more than 50 per cent of all new construction, business expansion and progress during the past decade has been effected by depreciation. If an individual uses a car both for business and pleasure he will have tax troubles depreciating his vehicle in the manner he would like to. But the corporate executive who uses his company car also for a mobile bedroom doesn't worry. The rental comes right off the top. And Uncle Sam goes for about half the tab—including the entertainment.

In any event speculators who seek to acquire wealth by leveraging money market instruments of the United States government, or try to make killings by forward hammering of our dollar on a shoestring basis (10 per cent of the funds involved) should do a whale of a load of studying and prior preparation. McGraw-Hill has published a book on government securities for $12.50, including mathematical formulas. Designed primarily for bond dealers, this book does reveal a mathematical approach to yields, etc. First Boston and Morgan Guaranty both publish free booklets every other year explaining all the money market instruments of our government—and these should be thoroughly examined before making commitments. Do *nothing* without expert guidance and an advance knowledge of both costs and risks. Government securities may be carried on margins as low as five to ten cents of the dollar value purchased. The commissions are ridiculously cheap (62½ cents a Treasury Bill of $1,000 face, and $1.25 a bond) and the debt instruments may be both bought and margined at commercial banks or members of the New York Stock Exchange.

Money Market Pros

Finally, it should be remembered that in dealing in government securities the leverage operator is pitting his skill against the people who make the market: the pros. Everything that goes in the government market is traded over-the-counter, so when the leveraged profit-seeker buys, he buys from a principal and when he sells, he sells to a principal. Naturally, private individuals are permitted to partake in part of the private auction that is held at the New York Fed. each week, but the convenience of having bond dealers who are also members of the New York Stock Exchange do this makes the minute savings of the commissions involved in buy-it-yourself Treasury Bill trading ludicrous. Charles Quincey & Co., founded in the

19th century, is one of the few New York Stock Exchange firms on Manhattan's toe that deals mainly in money market instruments for private accounts. Firms like Salomon Brothers do mainly an institutional business, making markets for other brokers and dealers as well.

The reason federal regulations permit investors to buy government securities with five cents on the dollar of the investment is that the securities are extremely liquid, do not fluctuate too violently (except in times of sudden interest change) and help Uncle Sam pay his obligations. But the reason the regulations demand 80 per cent margin on listed issues is to prevent and forestall "too much" speculation.

···· 11 ····

Real Estate Leverage

A survey of the literature on the subject of real estate turns up a myriad of books slanted toward telling the public how to make a million or more in real property operations. There is, of course, no law against ownership outright (all cash) of real property, but the genuine fortunes of the past decade in this connection have been made with other people's money.

Find a Property

The simplest form of profit in this direction comes from finding a property, finding someone who can use the property and putting the principals together. My friend Max has made a small bundle in this fashion. He looks at a lot in a certain town—and finds out who owns it. "How much do you want for the lot?", he asks. The answer is usually, "I have to be crazy in the head to sell it with land values rising each day. But if some lunatic wanted it for $10,000 I might sell it."

Now Max knows people who build gas stations and operate them. He approaches a prospect and says—in a whisper: "I got a lot. A beauty. Twist my arm and you can have a fantastic location for $15,000."

The avidity of the gas station builder-operator is boundless. He knows if the location is good a bank will look after most of the cost of the land, so he takes a ride with Max, likes the location and offers Max $13,500 for the property. Max acts wounded and says he'll let the prospect know in 24 hours.

Immediately thereafter he scurries over to the genuine owner of the lot and says, "The price you ask ($10,000) is too high. But give me a thirty-day option to buy it at $9,500 and I'll pay you $200 for the option."

The lot owner is firm. After all he smells that Max may have something up his sleeve so he says, "No. I'll give you the option, but the price is $10,000." So Max counters, "O.K. But the option money must be reduced from the price of the lot when title is taken."

Max pays the $200—and gets a bona-fide option to buy the lot in question for the next month at a price of $10,000 (less the $200 option cost). *And now he owns the lot as if he had actually bought it.*

So he goes back to the gas-station constructor and makes a deal to sell the lot for $13,500. Assuming that the deal is consummated, how does Max stand?

Gross profit on lot=	$3,500
Legal fees, etc. =	500
Before tax profit =	$3,000

Now suppose that after paying for the option, Max finds the developer of high-priced gas stations has changed his mind and doesn't want the lot after all. What is the worst that can happen? By virtue of his option, Max can scurry around for the next few weeks trying to palm off at a profit the lot somebody else owns and has to pay taxes on. Shrewd real estate operators have made fortunes via the option method—and, of course, in cases where they lost, their loss was confined to the actual expense of the option. In Max's case the *most* he could lose would be $200.

Development Fortunes

One of the best real estate novels of all time, describing the operations of a developer, is *Kane's World*, Simon & Schuster, 1968. Here a novelist who has had long experience in the real estate field narrates the happenings to a high-powered developer of the Zeckendorf type. It chronicles his trials and triumphs with builders, contractors, banking interests, tenants, etc. But most of all it indicates that anyone who is insane enough to assume the responsibility of making a building come to life from the ground up takes the risk of dying from a heart attack. So for most readers—and indeed for the majority of people seeking leverage—the best suggestion they can ever receive is to let somebody else do the *aggravation* part of the real estate business: construction and development. The same suggestion applies to finding lots and properties; tying them up and reselling them via option or ownership methods. So what is left? *Leverage.*

In this respect the sophisticated speculator deals solely with income property which is already mortgaged.

Assume that an office building is 85 per cent rented, and is mortgaged for $1,000,000 on a 6 per cent situation with 19 years to run. The building throws off—after mortgage payments —$100,000 a year. Normally, the seller will capitalize the building at ten times the cash flow above the mortgage, so that a person paying $2,000,000 for the property is paying the owner $1,000,000 for the mortgage and ten years anticipated income generated by the property.

Mortgage Recasting

The operator who finds such a situation and can arrange a deal to buy this building on these terms probably has—in advance—made arrangements with some bank or other lending agency to "recast" the mortgage back to 25 or 30 years at a 7 per cent interest rate. He can also buy this $2,000,000 property with $300,000 of his own money. Now as soon as title is taken and the mortgage has been recast, the payments on the mortgage have been substantially reduced by virtue of the longer maturity of the mortgage —and the *cash flow* of the building has been *materially increased.*

So, then, under the terms of the new financing —and with the operator succeeding in renting some of the 15 per cent available space, even at discounts—he may build the cash flow up to

$150,000 a year, after expenses and mortgage payments. What does he do now? Obviously, by virtue of a $150,000 cash flow he can capitalize it at $1,500,000 over the existing mortgage, using the ten-times-leverage rule. So he may offer the building for sale at *nine* times its cash flow, an obvious bargain. How does he make out if he sells on these shortly after purchase? Eliminating consideration of lawyers' fees, and other charges including transfer taxes, he will have grossed a half million dollars on his $300,000 "seed money" (money needed to swing the deal to begin with).

Understandably, swinging a deal like this cannot be done by a small-time operator who seeks to option a lot or a building for resale to somebody else, because even if the operator who managed to recast his mortgage cannot sell it at nine times leverage to somebody else, it will take *two years* for him to pull out his $300,000 and look for another office building to refinance. From the third year on—assuming the tenants remain at the same rentals—the leveraged operator is making a gross of $150,000 a year cash flow with *no investment*. Why anybody ever tries to speculate in the stock market is simply beyond the ken of this author who devoted 30 years to the market without knowing such happenings occurred in the realm of real estate.

Suppose the operator in the previous example did not recast the nineteen-year mortgage but was content to go along with existing conditions; his "seed money" would have come home to him in three years. Now a knowledgeable operator would have lined up occupants for the 15 per cent unoccupied space in the building even before he took title. In that event, of course, the cash flow of the building under the existing mortgage conditions would have been materially increased. So that assuming the operator managed to line up another $35,000 in annual rentals he could refinance the mortgage for more than $2,000,000, to say $2,350,000—and immediately pull out his seed money of $300,000+ plus $50,000 of bank money for use elsewhere. Not only does he now immediately own a building without *any* investment, but he also has an extra 50 grand to leverage something else! This process of "mortgaging yourself out" is one of the best tools available to the leverage operator. It is also one of the most dangerous. With the property mortgaged to the hilt, a ten per cent drop in occupancy will force the operator to bring back some "money from home." And if the money from home is not readily available, because it has been tied up in something else, the property may have to be subjected to a distress sale situation—causing a severe loss.

Building a Second Income

Probably no real estate operator in history lived on the knife of this kind of leverage as long or as actively as William Zeckendorf. But when conditions went against him, he wound up in a bankruptcy action in excess of $58 million of debt against about $2 million in assets—and with ten per cent of his annual $35,000 salary garnisheed by creditors. For a fascinating, step-by-step account of how one man who started with very little money wound up with a fortune in real estate deals, do not fail to read *How to Use Leverage to Make Money in Local Real Estate*, by George Bockl, Prentice-Hall, 1965. But George Bockl is a real estate broker of long standing, and he operates in Milwaukee. Operating in New York City or any other city involves the same principles, but perhaps the competition is keener.

In any event it does make a good deal of sense for anyone in their "medianetic" age (45 to 60) to look into the possibilities of building a first or second fortune from leveraging real estate. And for those in the geriatric category (a nasty connotation applied to people 65 and over who are today considered by government and corporations alike as too old to do anything but collect money) there seems to be nothing as fascinating as putting together real estate deals either as a broker or as an investor.

The reason people in their forties may be more successful at the intriguing game of getting rich on other people's money is that by the time they reach that age they may already have racked up a record of financial achievement, solidity, honesty, reliability and all the other Boy Scout attributes necessary to get a bank or savings and loan institution to extend the needed mortgages for leveraged real estate operations. Despite what doubting Charleys might say, money lenders are primarily as much interested in the character of the borrower as they are in the ability of the borrower to repay or amortize his loan via cash flow considerations.

This has been particularly true in the case

of banks that lend money to builders to develop land by erecting housing projects.

Real Property—And Banks

In this regard a stunning financial success occurred from 1960 to 1968 in the case of a New York State senator. In 1960, his net worth was about $30,000. But by the end of 1968 he had amassed several millions of dollars after taxes through perfectly legal methods of making a fortune in real estate development by getting rich on other people's money. In this case, the other people's money was bank money.

According to reports, this senator's fortune began when an aggressive builder came to him, took him in as a partner, and the senator arranged for financing for the venture by obtaining unsecured loans from a local bank. Backed by these "character" loans, the venture flourished so that during the eight-year period the pair managed to borrow more than a million dollars in unsecured loans and more than $20 million in building loans and mortgage credits. Because of this the senator and his partner today control a real estate complex conservatively valued at $12 million, just as long as they don't have to sell it under distressed circumstances. But even though there is the suggestion that the banks extended the loans in the first place because the senator was a politician, the truth of the matter is that they granted the loans because they knew he was honest and would repay in kind. So Horatio Alger corn or not, banks will normally not lend unsecured or even secured money to a man they suspect of moral turpitude.

Form a Team

A sensible operator—any age group over 21 —assembles his team much in the manner of a general planning an assault on the hidden enemy. First and foremost he requires two dedicated (honest) servants: (1) a real estate broker; and (2) a lawyer. These are vital appurtenances to any successful speculator's situation in real property. Having found the proper parties to serve his interests while handing him bills for their own efforts, the operator *must* find financing sources for his operations.

In recent years, commercial banks have enlarged their participations in real estate financing. Savings and loan associations have been granted new powers to lend money outside their local areas. Savings banks and insurance companies are likely sources of leverage for real estate operations. And so it goes.

Political Help

Ownership of income-producing property often carries with it problems that can be solved by political help. For example, an enterprising soul bought a children's day camp at a fair price. He had as much intentions of operating a day camp at a profit as the author has of resettling near Baffin Bay. Soon after he purchased the camp the operator applied to the county for permission to build a huge swimming pool, complete with lockers and cabanas "for the children."

Immediately, the surrounding residents voiced their objections. They stormed and protested against the county giving the operator the "variance" he needed to build the pool. Religious organizations entered into the fray and there was a genuine teapot tempest for awhile. But because the camp owner was quite well connected in the fire department of the village he lived in, and because politicians will naturally favor people who vote for them and aid the party's campaign, the camp owner got the variance—and he built the pool.

A few years later, he filed for permission to operate cabana and pool club for adults, claiming he was losing his shirt in the children's camp business. The public storm again broke —and at this writing he still has not been favored by the politicians. But if I were a betting man I would wager that in the end he is going to win out—and eventually own and operate the cabana club, which was the main reason he bought the camp in the first place. Oddly enough, even if he does not win out, he hasn't lost anything. Right after the swimming pool was built he raised the tuition, hired a fine head counselor, converted the camp into an all-year-round nursery school, day school along with his summer camp bit—and the public supported the place to such an extent thereafter that the camp has shown a *profit* ever since!

Delicate Matters

In the past handful of years, the Long Island area has been wracked by series after series of scandals involving land grabs, conflict-of-interest and other unsavory items which make grist for the newspaper mills. Dealing with politicians has always been a delicate matter ever since the infamous tin box of a New York City sheriff made headlines so many years back. And anyone who intends to deal in real estate that may involve political favoritism is treading on an uncharted minefield. But regrettably politicians are an apparent fact of life in real estate operations.

The owner of a roller skating rink in a local Long Island area had been pestered by all kinds of civic groups to end his operations. Pressure had been applied for years on politicians to end the rink's operations by edict, but to no avail. Fortuitously for the neighborhood the rink burned down on a winter night. The operator, after collecting insurance applied for permission to rebuild his rink. The town officials refused. The situation became like the tug-of-war between the Russians and the United States about rockets during the last war. It turned out that the Russians wound up with better Germans than we did. In this case the rink operator fielded his own politicians and the fight was on. His victory was partly Pyrrhic. He was eventually permitted to build an ice skating rink. But little did he care. The banks looked after almost everything, and now the cash rolls in during all the months except summer. Before, when he operated the roller skating rink, it was closed from September to March.

You Can't Manufacture Land

It was my pleasure to become friendly a long time ago with a very humble, but extremely intelligent individual. This man started a business forty years ago in a loft in Queens and struggled through the Depression days in typical hierarchical management manner—as the "boss." But as his business prospered he avoided the stock market like the proverbial plague. Instead he put every extra dollar he could come by into land. Needless to say today he is a multimillionaire. At lunch recently in one of Long Island's poshest restaurants he leaned over the table and advised: "Buy land. It's got to go up in value because there is only just so much of it. You can't manufacture it. It doesn't wear out. And if it lies along the line of population expansion you have to get rich."

He also admitted that he would never have been able to amass his many millions if he didn't have support from friendly thrift associations and banks. It certainly is not seemly to suggest that this book become a guide to how to become friendly with a banker and melt his cold, cold heart to such an extent that he will unlock the vault for your benefit. But if people are interested in getting into development or management of real property, they can inflict no harm on themselves if they become buddy-buddy with the people who will have to make the decisions as to whether or not to extend that loan so necessary to swing the deal. Bankers and savings and loan officers are as human as anybody else in other lines of endeavor. They too might repay kindness, consideration, etc. with an "OK" at the right time. But the supplicant for the funds must be honest enough to clearly intend to make repayment on time at the time the loan is extended.

· · · · 12 · · · ·

Leveraged Retirement

Truly we live in an age of miracles. Our benign government presses social security, medicare, medicaid and other amenities upon the populace, but it does very little to look after the worsening rise in the cost of living. Regrettably, most senior citizens, and many middle-aged and junior citizens who happen to be in civil service with government, state or municipality, live on rather stable—and fixed—incomes. To offset the constant inroads made in the dollar, young people look for capital-gain hedges against inflation. But what can the oldster do? He *needs* return, extra income to offset increasing costs. He cannot wait for "the long pull."

Earning Power

If an elderly man is active, of course, he

can get a part-time or full-time job. He can, if qualified, teach, or sell, or write books. In any event, an active person has earning capacity. In like manner, the person's assets have *earning power*. The *first* thing any sensible person seeking extra income through earning power of his assets should do is take Elizabeth Fowler's advice: "Make up a personal balance sheet."

Actually the only time most of us find out how much we are worth is when we happen to run afoul of the Internal Revenue Bureau and are subjected to a net worth examination. So without the urging of the tax department or anybody else, sit down and make up a fair, complete statement. Recently a friend came to me to ask how he could make a little extra something because he could not manage on the income from Social Security and his savings. "Do you know your assets and liabilities?", I asked. He jumped as if stung and retorted, "Assets? Who's got assets? Bills I have, plenty."

But I decided to probe a bit further. And in the process caused this former professor of accountancy (not accounting) to prepare the following statement:

Assets		*Liabilities & Net Worth*	
Cash in savings banks:	$22,000	Merchants, rent,	$ 5,000
Common stocks:	$28,000	Net worth	$45,000
Total assets:	$50,000	Total	$50,000

He also was receiving $180 a month from the government and $350 a month from his pension, so that his income and expenses looked like this:

Income:

Interest on savings $1,100

Dividend income	840
Retirement fund	4,200
Social Security	2,160
Total income	$8,300

Expenses:

Rent	$4,200
Utilities	600
Food	1,600
Clothing	400
Books	1,500
Other	2,000
	$10,300

Obviously, if the professor eliminated the expense item under "other" he would just about be able to squeak through on an even keel. But the "other," which at first he adamantly refused to reveal, evidently represented a necessity. And in order to meet that obligation he practically killed himself writing, doing occasional lecturing, proof-reading and compiling indexes. But to his credit he managed to make that extra two grand each year to supply him with the wherewithal for the mysterious entry "other."

And it was to forestall his continual "slavery" that he sought my counsel.

The first thing I did was attack his expenses. He agreed to move from his Park Avenue apartment to a residential hotel in the neighborhood for similar accommodations at $180 a month, making his rent $2,160 instead of $4,200. Books were evidently part and parcel of his lonely life so I did not chop there. And, of course, he would not divulge what the $2,000 expense for other was—and he at the time was 78!

Meanwhile, all but $5,000 was extracted from the bank, and bonds were purchased to yield him 8 per cent instead of 5. The increase in income represented $1,350 in additional cash flow. This made the ex-professor literally jump with joy, and now he chortled, "Gracious. I can spend another $1,350 a year at least on stamps!" *Now* I knew what his "other" expense was. And I pressed him for the details of his stamp collection.

It turned out that this professor possesses the most complete collection in the world of the stamps of Colombia. The stamps are valued somewhere in the neighborhood of $300,000. The collection was amassed by many years of buying, swapping, struggling, etc. But having a value of $300,000 today it will surely be worth some half a million in a few years.

I blew my cork. "Professor," I screamed, "Sell the damn stamps and convert them into 8 per cent investments. You can then add thousands of extra dollars a year to your income after taxes; live on Park Avenue and see the world too."

He impaled me with a glance that was at the same time filled with pity and scorn. "My boy," he whispered, "How can I sell them? I don't know what the collection cost me, and I couldn't possibly come up with a suitable figure for the tax department. Besides, I'd rather die than part with my stamps."

About Older People

Earlier in this book I mentioned that there are more nuts walking around outside than inside the looney bins. But some of them are lovable. I didn't press the issue, but this oldster

can happily grow older in peace as he hoards—
and collects—his precious stamps.

Because older people have probably made
some sort of better than casual connections with
bankers during their lifetimes, chances are they
can participate in loans on real property more
readily than younger people.

In recent years a rash of condominium housing has erupted around the Miami Beach area.
The people who flock to buy these apartments
range between 65 and older. Many of them
even lie about their age. But those who eventually buy the apartments receive long-term
mortgages. The likelihood of the owners living
to pay off this kind of mortgage is remote, so
they pay a heavy fee for insurance. In any
event, those who retire to the sunny South to
live in a condominium generally have managed
to generate enough cash flow to meet their needs.
If not they either have to depend on their relatives and children, or move.

Everyone who has assets can increase the
yield on them and keep a similar degree of
safety. Why do thousands of people all over our
country run to the bank or savings and loan
association which is insured by an agency of
the federal government and are content to
receive 5 per cent per year compounded quarterly, when they could actually buy obligations
of the United States government that will yield
much more? And can buy securities of agencies
of the government that will pay as much as
8 per cent?

The answer might be the same as the one
applied to those deluded souls who save in a

Christmas Club account at their bank, receive no interest and get their own money back at the end of the year, when the bank has had the use of it for free—and had the club depositors maintained passbook accounts, they would have *earned* interest on their weekly deposits and had that much more to spend on Christmas. In essence these are *stupid* people.

Sensible Financial Planning

A sensible planner in the field of personal finance keeps *only* enough safe money to provide for possible emergencies. The rest must work for him or for her. How a person makes his financial bed while he is working predicates the way he will rest in it when he retires. And leverage often makes the difference between silk sheets and pillow cases—and muslin.

· · · · 13 · · · ·

Rear-View Leverage

A book takes longer to turn out than baking a cake. And even in this sliding age of instant publishing it takes quite a bit of time from conception of any good book until it is published. In the case of this work, my effort began in the summer of 1968, when margin regulations were 70 per cent. And as I worked along fleshing out the skeleton of this book, margins were hiked to 80 per cent. Why? Well, Washington evidently became alarmed at the efforts of the Dow-Jones to break 1,000 on the upside and decided to dampen the speculative spirit which seemed to run through the nation's markets at the time. Later, margins were dropped to 65 per cent.

And so I was caught in a pickle, let alone a trauma, trying to alter this book so it would be current at the time it made

its debut. As I struggled along, inwardly re
senting the restrictions placed upon speculators by the Administration's harsh credit rules
as expressed in Regulations T&U and the
burdensomely unfair Regulation G, the stock
market began to decline. Down, down, down
it went as the country began to feel both the
effects of a money squeeze by the Federal
Reserve and a recession due to more reasons
than this book has room to explain. Certainly
in a country in which the cost of living was
suddenly rising at an alarming rate, despite the
face of a business recession, it seemed logical
to some that the prices of stocks would keep
rising. Instead they have kept declining—making in the process unprecedented opportunities
for the use of rear-view leverage.

20/20 Hindsight

Now precisely what is rear-view leverage?
Briefly it is an able exercise in 20/20 hindsight
in which a person with cash can take advantage
of the built-in leverage occasioned by a severe
stock market decline.

For example, 1969–1970 played havoc with
a certain breed of companies called conglomerates. These conglomerates grew to power by
takeovers and acquisitions, by mergers and
liquidations occasioned by aggressive management aided by bank loans and other financial
angles. So that Whittaker Corporation, for
example, which last year traded as high as 31
is currently trading at 9. Glen Alden, hitting
a high last year of 21 is currently about 6. And
so it goes.

Naturally a cash investor purchasing 100 shares of Whittaker at the high of last year would be suffering a $2,200 paper loss but he would still have his stock. And chances are he would be anxiously watching the stock quotations for a "rebound," so that once Whittaker "came back" to where he was about even he could "get out with his skin." The same situation may probably be safely applied to people who unfortunately took a position in Glen Alden at 21 and averaged by buying more shares when it dropped to 17. Locked in at the 6 level, they too must be waiting to get even.

Of course, these hypothetical investors may be more real than imaginary, because even though I have spoken to thousands of investors during the past two years, I have still to find any who have made a buck during this last market decline. And during 1969 there wasn't a single significant mutual fund that managed to demonstrate a profit while their managers were managing other people's money.

It all sounds pessimistic, but going all the way back to the buttonwood tree where it all began in the 18th century, only optimists have managed to consistently rack up stock market or real estate profits in the USA.

So let's think optimistically.

Comeback Stocks

Go down through the list of good New York Stock Exchange stocks and jot down issues which have declined more than 60 per cent from their 1969 highs. You will be both surprised and astounded. Now just for practice assume that you did go out and buy 100 Whittaker at 9—and pay for it in cash. You would be swinging what was formerly $3,100 worth of equity for a measly $900. It seems to me that only eggs in the supermarket can duplicate such value. My wife just bought three dozen medium-size eggs for 29¢ a dozen.

Now assume you want to go after larger things like good blue chips. Some digging and price comparisons here will also reveal tremendous discounts from what other investors paid last year. Moreover, the risk of using leverage in greatly depressed quality issues is already lessened by the price drop. And as a new crop of investors reach the market every five years or so good stocks will come back. Who says so? I do. And I ought to know because I have lived through activity in the stock market since 1937 and have researched the stock market thoroughly all the way back to the nineteenth century when the coal hole merged with the burnt-out members to form the present stock exchange in New York City.

So when does genuine opportunity knock in the rear-view leverage department? The answer just might lie in the signals sent out by the Federal Reserve Board. Robert Stovall, a partner in Reynolds & Company, says, "The Fed's timing has usually been pretty good. Since World War II there have been six reductions in the margin rate. With the exception of 1953, each reduction caught the market close to its bottom. This shows Washington does have its eye on Wall Street."

Now whether or not Mr. Stovall's observation can be applied to the present chaotic condition in Wall Street may be debatable. But the facts are that Standard & Poor's 500-stock index fell some 25.7 per cent from December 1968 to May 1970. The decline from January to October 1966 (the year of the tight money) was 22.1 per cent and the decline in the S&P index from December 1961 to June 1962 (the Kennedy Krash) was 28 per cent. In each of the previous declines dating all the way back to 1946, the market has *always* come back stronger than ever. As an irrepressible optimist I do believe that it will come back again strongly in the near future. But only if interest rates are reversed in trend and earnings begin to again take the place of operating losses.

Make It with Bonds

So what did I do after the Fed recently reduced the margin from 80 per cent to 65 per cent? Truthfully, I bought no stock. But my wife gobbled up a bunch of Glen Alden bonds due in 1988 at a price under 50. For each $1,000 face-value bond purchased at less than $500 she should receive (until 1988) $60 a year interest in two annual payments. And in 1988, if Glen Alden is still in business and meets its debt when it becomes due, she will receive a capital gain of more than $500 per bond. Now why did she do this?

Even after lecturing her loud and long about the depressed state of the market she decided to *triple* her money between now and 1988 (18 years), and she chose these bonds to do the job. Her figures are:

```
Investment per bond, 1970 .......... $500
Interest 18 years at $60 per year ....1,080
Long-term capital gain .............  500
```

So smiling sweetly at me she proved that, not considering taxes, each $500 she committed in 1970 should return her $1,580 by 1988.

Now what if the company defaults, cannot pay the interest, God forbid, and the bonds keep going down in price? Well, at the rate I have to labor in order to make ends meet in this inflationary age, I think that's going to be a concern of my wife's next husband.

In the meantime, you too can apply rear-view leverage to the bond list. For example, if you don't like Whittaker stock there is a bond issue which came out in 1968 at 100 (which of course means $1,000) and the bonds currently are selling at 45 (which means $450 per bond). Since these bonds pay $45 a year, the current return is about twice as large as bank interest —with the chance for a $550 long-term capital gain by 1988, the year these bonds mature.

Now since bonds can be leveraged by a deposit of 25–30 per cent, the advantages of purchasing such rear-view leveraged securities on margin are immediately obvious. In the case of the Glen Alden bonds, buyers can make money on the interest they are charged by the broker. By this I mean the investor who buys these bonds on margin and borrows money to partially pay for them has to pay his broker roughly 10½ per cent, while he is receiving 12 per cent from the Glen Alden security.

The speculators who leveraged according to the buy-higher-fool theory already have been broken and indeed busted—that is if they margined their purchases. So it becomes finally obvious that to succeed in getting rich with other people's money, the speculator must be alert enough to step into the market at approximately the right time and have sufficient resources or backers to be able to average or retain his position until times get better.

Tax Loss Benefits

The library shelves are crammed with stock market books that spout platitudes. Many years ago I wrote that successful speculation, leveraged or otherwise, depends at least 50 per cent upon luck. My associates in academe who program computers and thereby believe they are able to approximate future prices of securities have long since swallowed their taunts. And those who believed their computers cannot rightly say they have cushioned their loved ones in advance of their passing. So be alert. Jump at the profit opportunity an oversold market presents. Leverage to the hilt. And if you are successful, you too can buy that chateau in France, or that villa in Italy. If you are not lucky, you can always take a tax loss. In 1957 I suffered a $60,000 loss but could only offset it with $1,000 a year from income for the next five years. Unfortunate speculators who are hurt in this fashion today can take such a sum off for the next 60 years at $1,000 a year. But any corporation suffering such a loss can carry it over against earnings in an *unlimited* annual fashion. The obvious favoritism by the tax laws toward corporations over individuals is appalling. But that's another book for another season.

Good Luck. And remember: It's only money.

GLOSSARY

ACQUISITION: When a large company swallows up a smaller one, the result is called an "acquisition." But there have been cases in acquisitions where the canary swallowed the cat. Generally this kind of takeover offers plenty of profit opportunities for leveraged speculators. See: TAKEOVER.

BOOK VALUE: In business, the book value of a corporation is determined by subtracting from the tangible assets all the liabilities, including long- and short-term debt. The book value of an individual is what he owns minus what he owes. See: NET WORTH.

BUILT-IN LEVERAGE: Certain issues contain built-in leverage. For example conglomerate companies invariably have either bank debt or corporate paper outstanding. Then certain media like warrants, rights, puts and calls which control the action of underlying stock also have built-in leverage. For example, purchase of a warrant on credit provides extra leverage, because the warrant requires less out-of-pocket money than the purchase of the stock, yet logically should follow the pattern of the stock's prices.

BUYING POWER: Margined or cash securities which appreciate in price create paper profits. Investors can use these unrealized profits to buy more stock. To calculate the buying power in any account, divide the excess by the margin requirement. See: EXCESS.

175

CALLS: Contracts giving the buyer the right to purchase 100 shares of a specific stock at an agreed price for a set period of time. A call simulates a long position, with limited risk.

CASH ACCOUNT: The nature of an account at a brokerage firm wherein purchases are paid for in full within seven days after the purchases are made.

COMMODITIES: See: FUTURES.

CONVERSIONS: The process of changing a put into a call or a call into a put. This can only be accomplished with the cooperation of a put-and-call dealer and the exchange firm which acts as his conversion house.

CREDIT: This is one of the most confusing—and contradictory—terms in the English language. If one owns something, it is a credit to his balance sheet. And if one obtains a loan from a bank crediting his account, he owes instead of owns. Webster's reveals at least seven differing meanings of credit, but in this book credit is a sum of money placed at a person's disposal on either a short-term or long-term basis. To obtain credit one must usually have either a good set of financial statements, a good reputation, or both.

CREDIT BALANCE: The amount of cash in a bank or brokerage account which is unencumbered, free and clear and can be withdrawn on demand.

DEBIT BALANCE: The amount owing a broker in·a cash account and the amount of credit extended to an investor or speculator in a margin or general account.

DRAFT DELIVERY: This is the method banks and brokers use to buy or to sell securities. The bank or broker orders securities and after purchase instructs the seller to deliver said securities against payment to a bank or broker. This takes longer than the customary five-day clearance period and gives the buyer extra time to pay. Fed regulations permit up to 30 days for securities purchased via draft to be paid for. See: DRAFT KITING.

DRAFT KITING: A broker or other market operator orders stock from an American broker and instructs the buying broker to deliver the shares to a bank in another country. Meanwhile, if the shares go either up or down the "free rider" sells them at another American or foreign broker and instructs the selling broker to send a check to the draft kiter's bank in return for the sold-out shares. The bank that accommodates the kiter receives the bill from the buying broker and the confirmation and check for the sale from the selling broker. Thereupon the bank crosses the draft by paying the buying broker who presents the shares for payment and delivering the shares to the selling broker who has presented his check. After its charges, the bank either credits or debits the draft kiter's account with the monetary difference between the cost of buying and the proceeds of selling the shares involved in the draft. See: FREE RIDE.

EQUITY: For our purposes, this term signifies the money value of securities or real estate in any investor's portfolio less the loans outstanding against the securities or mortgages outstanding against the real property.

EXCESS: The excess in any margin account is the market value of the securities in the account, minus the debit balance (broker's loan), minus the required margin. See: BUYING POWER.

EXTENSION: The period of time granted by a lender to a borrower after the note or bond has become due and remains unpaid. Certain puts and calls can also be granted extensions of time past their contractual date by mutual agreement between the buyers and the sellers of the puts or calls in question.

FREE RIDE: Whenever a new issue of stocks or bonds is about to be launched on the unsuspecting investing public, the underwriter cannot pre-sell the shares or bonds. But he can obtain "indications of interest" while the issue is cooling off in the corridors of the SEC. Those who are lucky enough to "order" shares in advance via the indications of interest method often find that on the day the issue comes out of registration it shoots up to a premium above the original offering price. In that case the person who has been allocated shares by the underwriter can immediately sell out for a profit—without putting up a solitary dime. The process of profiting in this manner is called "free riding." Another method of doing this without being involved in underwritings is explained elsewhere in the glossary. See. DRAFT KITING.

FUTURES: Commodities which are traded for forward months are called "futures." Such commodities can vary from grains to hides and potatoes. Best thing about trading in commodity futures is that only a small deposit is required, no interest is extracted by the brokers for carrying the forward purchase and the commissions are far smaller for in-and-out transactions than they are for common stocks. See: HEDGING.

HEDGING: The process of protecting capital from loss by making off-setting transactions. Thus hedgers in the stock market might buy the shares of one steel company long and sell the shares of another steel company short. In commodity markets, spreads and straddles are resorted to. See: SPREADS, STRADDLES.

HOUSE RULES: There are federal and Exchange rules which regulate minimum margins for various types of securities. They also have minimum deposits to safeguard brokers who endorse contracts for clients. But while the brokers must conform to the minimums set up in the rules, they can demand *more* than these minimums as protection from their customers. In other words, these brokers, members of private clubs, can demand whatever they want from their customers if they feel they are liable to get hurt. Thus if the minimum margin for the sale of a put option is 25 per cent, the broker who has to endorse the contract can demand 100 per cent. And he may arbitrarily refuse to endorse puts in any specific issue if he is worried about the state of the company concerned.

INITIAL MARGIN: This is the required amount of deposit which has to be placed in a margin account at a brokerage house or bank in order to comply with federal regulations. See: REG. T & U.

LEVERAGE: A latter-day synonym for credit. When a corporation's capitalization consists merely of common stock it has no leverage. But when it floats bonds it obtains credit and thereafter is considered to be leveraged. See: PERSONAL LEVERAGE.

LOAN: Whenever a man or institution with money hands money to a person or institution asking for it for a specific period of time the transaction is termed a loan. Thus a loan involves not only the giving of money, but also the promise on the part of the borrower to repay. In most instances the loan also involves interest payments to the lender as an inducement for him to extend the credit to the borrower. And in some instances the borrower is compelled to add a sweetener in the form of an equity kicker for the lender.

MAINTENANCE MARGIN: When the portfolio in any margin account declines in value, the owner of the account will be asked to deposit more margin to protect the brokerage house carrying the account. The same is true at banks carrying special-purpose or call loans for customers.

MARGIN: The monetary or securities deposit by any investor to secure adequately the stockbroker or bank extending credit in connection with the purchase of securities for said investor, or in connection with a short sale or option endorsement for said investor by a member firm of the New York Stock Exchange. See: LOAN; CREDIT; MARGIN ACCOUNT.

MARGIN ACCOUNT: The kind of customer's account at a broker where the purchases are partly paid for by money borrowed from the broker by the customer. The loan extended by the broker to the customer represents the customer's debit balance. See: DEBIT BALANCE.

MERGER: When one company marries another and both are more or less equally significant, the marriage is called a merger. If the marriage is made between a small firm and a large one in which the small firm emerges as the successor, it is called a "takeover." But when a small firm is gobbled up by a large one, the merger is called an acquisition. See: ACQUISITION.

NET WORTH: The net worth of an individual is all his assets such as cash, stocks, bonds and real estate, paintings, coins, stamps, etc., less whatever he may happen to owe via mortgages, debit balances to brokers and credit-card debt to banks. The net worth of a going corporation is the same as its book value. See: BOOK VALUE.

OPM: The initialism signifying "Other People's Money." See: CREDIT.

PERSONAL BALANCE SHEET: Everyone who files an income tax statement annually presents Uncle Sam with a personal profit-and-loss statement. But few people take either the time or the trouble to set down a balance sheet for their own edification of precisely what they own or owe. Try it today. And don't gasp at the results.

PERSONAL LEVERAGE: Application by an individual of the same kind of credit operations customarily entered into by corporations may be held to be personal leverage. See: CREDIT; OPM.

PORTFOLIO: Webster's defines the word portfolio in three different ways, including "a portable case for carrying papers or drawings." But the definition which applies in this book involves the securities held by any investor.

PROFESSIONAL: Anyone who plays the market for money might be termed a professional, but we mean only those who either make a living from the investing public or are dealers trading for their own accounts.

PUTS: Contracts giving the buyer the right to deliver 100 shares of a certain stock at an agreed, effective price for a set period of time. A put simulates a short sale, with limited risk.

PYRAMIDING: In Wall Street parlance, pyramiding is merely adding the buying power in a paper-profit situation to the purchase of more of the same or other paper. Trouble is, the danger to the risk-taker increases directly with the degree of pyramiding—especially if the pyramider does not have the reserves or the loan sources to maintain his position during bad markets.

REAR-VIEW LEVERAGE: Purchase of a greatly depressed issue in the hopes that it will rebound in price is called rear-view leverage. For example, in 1969 Whittaker was $31; in 1970 it was $9. A cash buyer at this level would have $22 worth of rear-view leverage.

REG. G: This is a ruling of the Federal Reserve Board—and upheld by a judge who deservedly went to his just reward—which extends the authority of the Federal Reserve Board to regulate the lending activities of unregulated money lenders.

REG. T: This is the regulation of the Federal Reserve Board which sets the rules for buying of securities on margin through regulated brokers and dealers.

REG. U: This is the regulation of the Federal Reserve Board which sets the rules for buying securities on margin through regulated banks.

RIGHTS. To satisfy the regulations about the preemptive rights of existing shareholders, most companies contemplating issuing new securities for capital purposes offer these new securities at lower-than-market prices to the existing shareholders first. This right to buy additional securities below the market becomes valuable because of the price differential, and the stockholder has the option of selling his rights for value, subscribing to the new issue, or letting the rights expire as worthless— an idiocy to say the least. Since rights last from two to eight weeks, generally the investing public must take action before the rights die. See: SUBSCRIPTION ACCOUNT.

ROLLING OVER: The process of exchanging a bond issue for another bond issue at maturity date. In this case, the holder of paper who is entitled to cash winds up with more paper but generally pays a higher interest rate. Rolling over its debt has been the major method of the post-Truman administrations in handling the debt that comes due each year. If the government had to pay out cash to meet its debt obligations it would go bankrupt *immediately*.

SPECIAL-PURPOSE LOANS: Under federal regulations banks can lend individuals only 35 per cent of the value of good stocks in order to use the money to buy more good stocks. But for loans collateralized by good securities and whose proceeds are going to be used for some good purpose other than buying good stocks, the government leaves it to the discretion of the lending institutions. Thus a borrower seeking to fix his roof can borrow 75 per cent of the value of 100 shares of AT&T for this special purpose, but he can borrow only 35 per cent of the value of his Telephone shares if he wants to buy more Telephone with the proceeds of his loan. Borrowers under the special-purpose "thing" must sign a statement attesting they are not going to use the loan money to buy stock. Penalty for lying to the government in this direction could be as much as two years in jail and a $10,000 fine.

SPECULATION: The attempt to profit from price changes. These changes can occur in bananas, steel, the stock market, the real estate market, etc. But wherever the changes occur someone is buying and someone is selling. On the NYSE someone can even go short (sell what he doesn't even own). In speculation someone wins and someone loses, but the banks and brokers always come out ahead because they charge for the use of money and services. Looking back over America's panic-riddled past it becomes immediately obvious that if we were born in the womb of revolution and raised on the milk of speculation, we are still suckling at the same breast right now.

SPREADS: In commodity futures trading the purchase of one month's future and the sale of another month's maturity in the same future is termed a "spread." Selling oats, for example, and buying corn constitutes a "straddle." Speculators maneuver with spreads and straddles because of lenient margin regulations, and their profit involves either a narrowing or a widening of the monetary differences in the prices of the commodities hedged via spreads and straddles. In the world of puts and calls, the term "spread" signifies a combination option in which the effective price of the put and the effective price of the call are different.

STANDBY SYNDICATES: These are groups of investment bankers who guarantee companies issuing rights in a stock subscription that if the existing stockholders and speculators who dabble in the rights do not subscribe to the involved shares, then the members of the standby syndicate will buy all the unsubscribed shares. Understandably, the exchange and the SEC permit the standby syndicate to legitimately manipulate the market (professors call it "stabilization") so that the rights will have value until the very last minute and people will be induced to subscribe.

STRADDLES: In commodity futures trading, the purchase of one commodity and the sale of another commodity constitutes a straddle. The purchase of September eggs and the simultaneous sale of December eggs represents a spread and not a straddle. In the world of puts and calls, a straddle is a combination option consisting of a put and a separate call at the same effective price which are sold as a unit.

STREET NAME: When shares are registered in the names of stock brokers in order to facilitate delivery and clearance they are called "street certificates" and the shares are said to be in "street name." All shares in margin accounts or which are hypothecated for loan purposes are in street name to make it easy for the creditor to dispose of the shares if the borrower defaults.

SUBSCRIPTION ACCOUNT: Unlike other accounts at New York Stock Exchange member firms, the *special subscription account* permits stockholders, who receive or buy rights to subscribe to additional shares in companies listed on that exchange, to actually buy the shares by paying only 25 per cent of the total price instead of the required 65 per cent initial margin required by law. The owner of a special subscription account must, however, margin his account fully within the next nine months after purchase, in three increments. Thus for three months after opening a special subscription account, the leveraged operator can ride the market and sell out without putting up more than his initial 25 per cent deposit.

TAKEOVER: When a small, aggressive corporation, well-schooled in bootstrap finance buys control of a large corporation, the process is called a "takeover." Generally it all begins with a confidential deal to buy the controlling block of stock and upon agreement with the controlling interests the acquiring corporation makes a tender offer to the existing shareholders in order to comply with the shareholders' preemptive rights. Takeovers usually offer unique opportunities for short-term profits.

TENDER OFFER: Commonly termed "tender," this is an advertised offer to existing stockholders for the purchase of their shares by an acquiring party in a merger or acquisition maneuver. Generally tender offers are priced sufficiently above the going market to induce shareholders to part with their shares, and thus with their votes.

WARRANTS: These are certificates generally issued in connection with bonds and debentures which offer the owners the privilege of subscribing to additional stock in the subject corporation at a price *above* the current market. This is the reverse of the terms of rights offerings which permit purchase *below* the market. The reason warrants have value, however, is that the privilege they carry generally is long-term, and in some cases perpetual.

WHEN ISSUED: When a stock has split and the old shares are trading, very often the new shares, which have not yet been actually printed by the corporation, also trade on a "when-issued" basis. This means that the buyer of the new shares can contract to purchase them but doesn't have to pay for them until they **are** delivered. In the case of purchase of when-issued shares at member firms, the purchaser must pony up a deposit of at least 25 per cent of the value of his purchase—and then bring his account up to cash or margin levels when the shares stop trading on a when-issued basis. The longest time shares traded within the author's memory on such a basis was Studebaker, which a handful of years back traded for about a year on a when-issued basis while its "old" stock also traded at the same time on a regular basis.

INDEX

A

Account switching, 70
Active commodities, list of, 77–78
American Cancer Society, 81
American Motors, 73–74
American Stock Exchange (all except), 51
American Telephone and Telegraph Company
    (AT&T), 16, 45–48, 59–60, 126
Antiques, 119
Art mania, 122–123
Art works, 119

B

Bache & Co., stockbrokers, 84
Baffin Bay, 155
Bahamas Islands, 57–58
Baltimore & Ohio Railroad, 40
Banco Financiero, 27
Bankers, 158

Barclay's Bank, 57
Barnes, Dr. Leo, educator, economist—and author, 39, 71
Baruch, Bernard, financier, 41, 74
Biltmore Hotel, 131
Black Watch Herds Corporation, 94
Bockl, George, author, 139–140 153
Borrowed-money game, 58
Built-in leverage, 31
Buying power, 62–63, 66–67

C

Call Power, 42
Calls, 31–32, 41
Canadian banks, 55–56, 61
Canadian brokers, 29, 51, 55
Cartwheels, 117
Cash:
　buying power, 71
　flow projection, 17–21
　generation, 67–68
　withdrawal power, 71
Castro, Fidel, communist, Cuban, 27
Charles Quincey & Company, 145
Colombia, 162
Commodities futures, 31, 74, 75–78
Continental Congress, 133
Conversion money, 102
Conversion power, 97–110
Conversions, 100–104
Cow club, 90–92
Cow deals, 89–96
Credit loopholes, 26–27
Cuba, 59
Currency hedging, 139, 142
Current equity, 71
Cutten, Arthur, trader, 86

D

Darvas, Nicolas, author and financier, 73
Day trading, 52–53
Debt instrument mix, 134–135
Dollar erosion, 143
Downside insurance, 132
Double-the-Money Table, 24–25
Dow-Jones Industrial Average, 165
Draft delivery, 54
Draft kiting, 55

E

Earning power, 159
Egg futures, 33–35
Excess, 71
Extensions, 106–107

F

Federal margin regulations, 59, 70
Federal Reserve Board, 109, 113, 168
Feed-lot fortunes, 90
Financial planning, 164
First Boston Corporation, investment bankers, 145
Foreign trades, 30
Fowler, Mrs. Elizabeth, *New York Times* financial writer—and author, 160
Free riding, 27, 53

G

Glen Alden, 53, 166–167, 169–170
Green & Ladd, stockbrokers, 106

H

Harper, Marion, advertising executive, 92–93
Harris Upham & Co., stockbrokers, 105
Havana Stock Exchange, 27
Hedging, 75–77
Hoarding, 111–124
Hornblower & Weeks, stockbrokers, 105
House rules, 60–61
How to Use Leverage to Make Money in Real Estate,
    153
Hutton, E. F. & Co., stockbrokers, 84

I

Internal Revenue Service, 58

J

Johnson, President Lyndon B., 81, 110, 112, 117

K

Kane's World, 149
Kennedy, President John F., 111
Kennedy "Krash," 169
Kidder, Peabody, stockholders, 106
Kroll, Dannon & Company, commodities brokers, 80

L

Leverage, 22–23
    factor, 38
    logic, 28

media, 31–44
  sources, 45–64
  summary, 42–43
Leveraged retirement, 159
Leveraged triple play, 72–74
Liechtenstein, 59
Listed leverage, 97
Live cattle, 87

M

Margin call, 59
Margin dispensations, 85
McGraw-Hill, publishers, 144
Merrill, Lynch, Pierce, Fenner & Smith, Inc., stock-
  brokers, 84, 105
Money market, 133–146
Montreal Stock Exchange, 51
Morgan Guaranty Trust Company, 145
Mortgage recasting, 150–152

N

National Association of Securities Dealers, Inc.
  (NASD), 52, 56
  member of, 62
New York Central Railroad, 15–16
New York Federal Reserve Bank, 145
New York Mercantile Exchange, 117
New York Stock Exchange (NYSE) (Big Board), 26–
  27, 32, 35–36, 49, 51–53, 55, 75, 97, 145, 167
  closings, 62
  margin, 59
  members, 70, 83, 95, 105
New York Times, The, 50, 93
Nixon, President Richard M., 118
Northern Miner, The, 51

O

Ontario Securities Commission, 52
OPM: Other People's Money, 16 *ff*
Over-the-counter house rules, 62
    strategy, 104

P

Paine, Webber, Jackson, and Curtis, stockbrokers, 62,
    84
Paper appreciation, 65
Pennsylvania Railroad, 15
Perfect leverage, 27
Personal leverage power, 15–30
Political help, 155–156
Prentice-Hall, publishers, 153
Price protection, 126
Protected leverage, 130
Protected profits, 125–132
Protective put, 107
Put-and-Call Bible, 40
Put-and-call course, 131
Put-and-call leverage, 32
Puts, 31–32, 41
Pyramid power, 62–63, 65–74

R

Real estate leverage, 147–158
Real estate option, 148–149
Rear-view leverage, 165–172
Regulation G, 58, 166
Regulation T, 46, 95, 166
Regulation U, 46, 166
Retirement, 159–164

Reynolds & Co., stockbrokers, 168
Rights, 31, 35–37
Roosevelt, President Franklin D., 133
Rose, Billy, impresario, 15, 41, 119

S

Saint Louis Cardinals, 50
Salomon Brothers, investment bankers, 146
San Diego Padres, 50
Sarnoff, Mrs. Paul, 169–170
Save by borrowing, 34
Savings and loan officers, 158
Schenley, Inc., 53
SEC: Securities and Exchange Commission, 51, 81
Shane, Jonathan, computer genius, 69–70
Shane's pyramid formula, 69–70
Silver certificates, 112
Simon & Schuster, 149
Sinclair Oil, 108
Smith, Adam (George Goodman), 59
Special subscription accounts, 37–38, 95, 97–99
Standard & Poor's 500-Stock Index, 169
Standard & Poor's *Stock Guide*, 40
Stock market insurance, 127
Stop-loss order, 127–128
Stovall, Robert, Reynolds & Co., luminary, 168
Straddling commodities, 85
Swiss banks, 57–58

T

Tel-Aviv Stock Exchange, 56
Thomas Haab & Botts, put-and-call dealer, 106
Tilden, Governor Samuel J., 120
Toronto Stock Exchange, 51
Treasury bills, 134–136
Truman, President Harry S., 133

U

University Computing, 28

V

Vineyard profits, 120–122

W

Wall Street Journal, The, 50, 92
Walston & Co., Inc., 84
Warrants, 31, 32
  checklist, 39
Western Union, 28
Whittaker, 166–167, 170
  bonds, 170
Wilson & Co., 77
Wine speculations, 121–122
World War I, 81
World War II, 81

Y

Your Investments, 39

Z

Zambian Stock Exchange, 56
Zeckendorf, William, leverage operator, 149, 152
Zelomek, A., economist, 81